AN AUSTRALIAN'S
CHILDHOOD IN CHINA

Neil Begley

An Australian's

CHILDHOOD

IN

CHINA

Under the Japanese

NEIL BEGLEY

Kangaroo Press

Cover design by Darian Causby

'There'll Always be an England' br R.Parker & H.Charles.
Lyrics reproduced by permission: © 1939 Dash Music Co. Ltd.,
8/9 Frith Street, London

First published in 1995 by Kangaroo Press Pty Ltd
3 Whitehall Road Kenthurst NSW 2156 Australia
P.O. Box 6125 Dural Delivery Centre NSW 2158
Printed by Australian Print Group, Maryborough 3465

ISBN 0 86417 739 9

To my wife Belinda who is there when I need her the most,
which is all of the time.

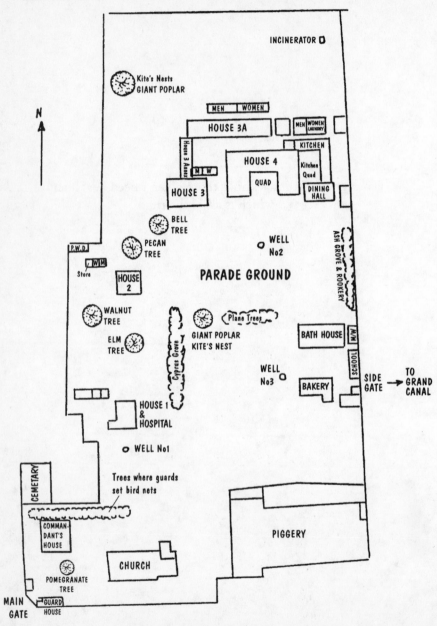

Rough Sketch Map of Yang Chow CAC "C"

CONTENTS

PRONUNCIATIONS

When I was in China, Chinese words could be written with the English alphabet by means of 'Romanisation', however this system did not give an accurate representation of how a word should sound, for example the name 'Chiang' is pronounced Jarng.

After the Cultural Revolution the Romanisation was abandoned and a new method of 'English style' writing call Pinyin was introduced. Whatever the reasons for introducing Pinyin, from a pronunciation view point it is, if anything, even further from a true phonetic representation.

In this book I have used neither of the above systems. Instead I have endeavoured, wherever possible, to spell any Chinese words as phonetically as I can.

FOREWORD

This book is not an historical record nor is it intended to be. These are my recollections which may well have been tempered by the passage of half a century. They are memories and as Jerome K. Jerome wrote in his 'Idle Thoughts of an Idle Fellow':

> That is just the way it is with memory; nothing that she brings to us is complete; all her toys are broken. I remember tumbling into a huge dusthole, when a very small boy, but I have not the faintest recollection of ever getting out again; and, if memory were all I had to trust to, I should be compelled to believe I was there still.

I have made no judgments nor drawn any in depth conclusions. I was only a young child. It is the story as I remember it, dustholes and all.

Neil Begley
1995

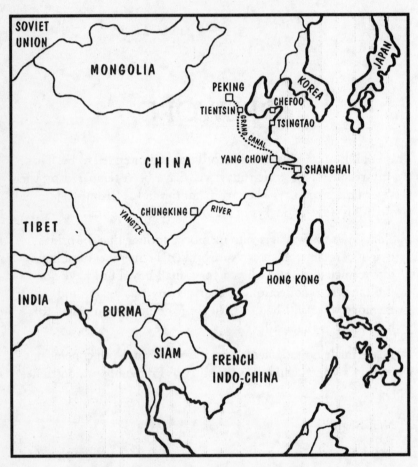

East Asia showing pre-war borders and names

CHAPTER 1

BORN IN PEKING

She sat on a low three legged stool in the middle of the floor of the servants quarters, dressed in the traditional garb of a Chinese peasant woman; black baggy trousers, black fabric shoes and a black cloth jacket fastened with buttons made from woven cord. Undoing the buttons she revealed two enormous yellow breasts with large brown nipples that protruded from two things that looked like lumpy ginger nut biscuits.

'Neeoo,' she called. 'Neeoo, lai-a.' Neil come here.

I'd toddle over to stand between her legs, facing her with my elbows resting on her knees. She smelt like a Chinese, they all smelt the same, not like we 'Foreigners' and, colour apart, I thought that smell was what made them different from us. Taking a nipple in my lips, I'd suck her warm milk while she ran her fingers through my long fair curls and crooned me haunting Chinese lullabies. She spoke only Chinese so I was more comfortable with Mandarin than I was with English and quite at home in the servants quarters with its plain table, rudimentary furniture, rough wooden stools and colourful crockery.

Chwan Tai Tai (Mrs Chwan) was my amah. I remember her as a plump, happy woman of indeterminate age with straight black hair pulled tightly back into a bun from her moon face that had a large flat nose, like a blob of squashed putty, in the middle of it. My mother would have been horrified if she'd seen me. My parents were missionaries, and as part of a contingent of about twenty Salvation Army officers, they'd set off by ship from Australia in 1921 to go to China. Chwan Tai Tai's ample breasts would not have been on the agenda of the education they had planned for me, their youngest child.

On their arrival in Peking, along with the other missionaries, they'd attended language school. By the time they were married two years later, having gained a reasonable grasp of Mandarin, they were sent into the interior to work amongst the villagers, where, as 'foreign devils', they were more of a curiosity than a necessity. Before setting off, Dad had done a crash course in medicine, so as the only 'doctor' for miles he opened a primitive clinic treating all sorts of ailments. He even performed the occasional minor amputation. After several months he contracted smallpox, a frightening disease for Foreigners but common enough amongst the Chinese. Soon he was delirious with fever but somehow Mum got him back to Peking in handcarts, donkey carts and, where there were rivers to cross, on flimsy sampans. He survived the trip and the ailment.

Shortly after my sister Audrey was born, in 1927, the family was driven out of China by the advance of the 'Reds', the communists under Mao Tse Tung. My parents went to India for five years during which time my brother Ian was born in Guntur, a small town near Madras. When China reopened to Foreigners they returned to Peking in 1932, where I was born by caesarean section at the German hospital after my mother had spent three days in labour. My birth was registered at the British Legation and bears the number 2. I haven't checked, but I suppose my sister would have birth certificate number 1. As Australians we were something of a rarity.

We lived in a small house called Ping Arn Farng (Home of Peace) which, like many in Peking, was one of a group of single storeyed terrace houses in an enclosed compound. They had packed earthen floors covered with a scattering of woven straw mats, 'Chinese style' tiled roofs and windows decorated with ornate fretwork. Instead of glass panes, the windows were covered with translucent white rice paper over mosquito netting. The paper could be rolled up like a blind to allow air flow through the house. The residents of the other houses were all missionaries and the only 'uncles' and 'aunties' that I knew.

In Peking the industrial revolution was still a long way off. Most districts had no reticulated water and no sewerage. Few houses had electricity so our cooking and heating was done by wood- or coal-burning stoves and our lighting was from kerosene lamps with tall glass chimneys and cotton wicks which, even after they were trimmed and adjusted gave off little more than a soft yellow glow. There was no plumbing. We bathed in a tin bath in water that we drew from large earthenware jars called karngs that stood outside each house.

Peking was a city of people. Labour was cheap—very, very cheap. All tasks were performed manually. Men loaded lorries by hand which were then pulled by other teams of men harnessed together with straw ropes. Men dug the roads and compacted them using heavy logs attached to several ropes. With a man holding each rope the logs were hoisted into the air then brought down with a dull thud. They would work like this for hour after hour, day in, day out. Heavy goods were carried in baskets suspended from poles across the shoulders.

There were hundreds of rickshaws which were the only form of public transport. They had rubber tyred wheels like bicycles but about twice the diameter, which frequently blew out with a bang like a rifle shot. Some had a bicycle bell attached to one of the shafts which was used to add urgency to the rickshaw boy's cries for right of way. Most had kerosene lights either side much like small coach lamps. Mounted at the rear were two steel brackets like inverted horns that curved down to about a foot above ground level. When the rickshaws were parked the shafts could be tipped up at the front so that the unit rested back on these supports. The brackets served another necessary purpose. When going uphill with heavy loads it was not unusual for the rickshaws to tip backwards onto these supports. The hapless rickshaw coolies with the shafts tucked firmly under their arms, would be lifted off the ground, legs kicking helplessly in the air. Rickshaw coolies usually wore cotton shirts open at the front and cotton trousers that came down just below the knees. Some were barefoot but most wore straw rope sandals which scuffed along the roads with a gentle swish, swish, swish as they ate up mile after mile at a steady jog trot. Some of the well-to-do Chinese had sedan chairs carried by private bearers but these were gradually being phased out and replaced with automobiles.

Water was delivered in wheelbarrows with large bamboo barrels lashed to their sides. The all-pervading sound of Peking was the squealing of wooden barrow wheels protesting against wooden axles. There were thousands of wheelbarrow coolies, collecting water from lakes, rivers and communal wells and delivering it throughout the city where it was tipped into the large earthenware karngs from which we dipped our water. One night when I was quite small our house caught fire. There wasn't a fire brigade to call, so a human chain was formed from our place to the nearest communal well and bamboo buckets of water were passed hand over hand to quench the flames.

Because of the risk of cholera, all drinking water had to be boiled—'Liang kai swai' it was called, cold boiled water. As well as cholera, we had to contend with typhoid fever and smallpox, so to keep these afflictions at bay we had regular 'shots'. Smallpox wasn't too bad, it was only a scratch on the arm, or on your leg if you were a baby, and if it 'took' the first time and developed into a sore full of pus, like a big boil, you didn't have to worry too much about it taking again with later vaccinations. But the needles for the others were a different kettle of fish. They'd give us a 'three in one' cholera, typhoid and paratyphoid shot with a needle about the size of a healthy crowbar stuck on the end on a huge glass syringe. The same needle would be used over and over again, so if you were well down the line it was pretty blunt by the time they plunged it into the muscle in the top of your arm. As if the jab wasn't bad enough, you could feel the stuff being pumped into you like gritty grains of sand. However, that was the easy part; next day you'd get a fever that climbed up around 103°F and your arm would swell up into a red welt that hurt like fury if anyone touched it. I've never had the diseases but I doubt they could be much worse than the needles.

Peking was a fascinating place enclosed by a city wall about thirty feet high and almost as thick. At Chen Mun—the main gate—there was an outdoor market like a rambling bazaar where you could buy anything from a thrush in an intricately carved bamboo cage or a whistling cricket, to a set of spectacles or a pair of fur gloves. The gloves often bore a remarkable resemblance to the family moggie which had strayed the previous week. There was another general market at Si Pilo—four arches (much like the arches you see in the Chinatowns of most big cities). But the best market was along dusty, unmade, potholed Pig Street, where you could browse through a seemingly limitless range of vegetables, live chickens, ducks and geese, large fish that swam in shallow open barrels, or pigs and goats. There were goldfish and rabbits and caged birds and magicians and jugglers and fortune-tellers with trained finches that would fly about to select your fortune from a box of prophesies. You bargained for everything with the stall-holders who shouted their wares over the noise of the squealing of pigs and the squawking of chickens which were being slaughtered and dressed by the side of the road where their blood pooled in the gutters. The stench was appalling, particularly in summer when Pig Street swarmed with flies. There were endless food stalls engulfed in the white mist that wafted up from bamboo rice steamers (most things in China were made from bamboo) and stands that sold a type of barley cake called manto, or white sticks of processed malt—my favourite treat, or bowsers, which were little mince meat and vegetable rolls wrapped in pastry rather like dim sims. When my mother walked along Pig Street she always held a handkerchief to her nose, but it was a great place for a little boy to visit.

There was no TB testing so we didn't drink cows' milk. Those who had the space kept a nanny-goat or two which the servants milked daily. If you didn't have a goat, milk vendors walked the streets leading mares, milking them on demand into a container. These horses were invariably followed by men with bamboo buckets tied to their backs and large ladles which they used to deftly scoop the manure up and over their shoulders into the buckets for use on their gardens.

Opposite the Pig Street market was the main coffin-maker's establishment where men worked in a sawpit with long crosscut handsaws, slicing tree trunks to be fashioned into rough caskets. Further down the road was a large earth mound full of ice. During the winter months, ice merchants cut blocks from the frozen rivers and lakes which they stockpiled and covered with layers of earth. The soil gave sufficient insulation to prevent the ice from thawing. When summer came, vendors dug it out and sold it to us to chill our iceboxes.

I loved the chaos that was Pig Street. It seemed to be one huge impenetrable traffic jam, cacophonous with the creak and groan of handcarts and squeal of barrow wheels against ungreased axles. Bicycle bells tinkled urgently and rickshaw boys shouted for right of way over the din of teams of labourers chanting 'Eiya ho, oawa ho, eiya ho, oawa ho', as they bent their backs under incredible loads. Frantic Chinese policemen with flaying truncheons tried vainly to establish some form of order.

Most of the better dressed Chinese men wore full-length grey, blue or black cotton gowns buttoned down the side and cotton trousers. Their feet were protected with cloth slipper-like shoes which disintegrated if they got wet, so the wearers were reluctant to go out in the rain. It was a funny thing about rain. The Chinese depended on it for their crops, for topping up their wells and for the floods that top-dressed their fields with alluvial silt. They watched the skies anxiously during droughts, burning incense and setting off firecrackers to appease the rain gods who conjured up the clouds. But in spite of this, however bad a drought may be, one must never ask a Chinese if he thought it might rain. That was a grave insult. The worst thing that you could call a Chinese was a tortoise—a wong ba—and the next great insult was a wong ba dan, a tortoise egg. It was claimed that a tortoise knew when it was going to rain because the back of its neck would sweat. If someone asked you if you thought it was going to rain, the inference was that you were a tortoise. I suppose that's logical!

Some men wore the traditional small black skullcaps with a red button on top, but on hot days most folk, men and women, wore large cone shaped woven bamboo 'coolie hats'. Chinese men placed great store on manual dexterity and consequently, when their hands were not otherwise occupied, to keep their fingers supple, they rolled a couple of walnuts over and over in their hands, making a rasping, grinding sound.

Boys and young men shaved their heads, though some left a small circle of hair at the back which they plaited into a long pigtail. It seemed to be the custom that only the old men grew beards, and these were mostly sparse and grey. The Chinese had a great respect for old age. It was considered that with age came wisdom, so old people were venerated.

Like Chwan Tai Tai, most women wore black baggy trousers and hip-length jackets that undid down one side at the front and were fastened with embroidered cloth buttons. Usually they wore their hair pulled back into tight buns. Many of the older women had bound feet. They hobbled along on what were little more than stumps, swaying their bodies to help propel themselves forward. I understand that the custom was introduced in the days of the Mongol incursions into North China at the time when the Great Wall was built. Apparently the raiders used to capture young women forcing them to run behind their horses as they dragged them away as booty. With Oriental cunning, the Chinese hit on the idea of binding baby girls' feet at birth so they couldn't run behind their captors. Incredibly the idea became fashionable and foot-binding was still practised as an aid to beauty centuries after the raids had ceased. In fact the mother of one of my amahs had bound feet. She'd once been a lady in waiting in the Forbidden City, to the Empress Dowager. I have a pair of her shoes, beautifully embroidered in silk, they measure four and three quarter inches (12cm) long.

The Chinese approach to hygiene was quite different from ours. They didn't use handkerchiefs; instead they blew their noses onto their fingers then wiped the snot on the nearest wall, post or tree trunk. Past masters of the art of spitting, they'd hawk deep in their throats and then eject an oyster-like dollop of phlegm. Where it landed was anyone's guess. As children we were always being warned to take care where we put our hands when we were out of doors. Chinese men urinated where and when the urge possessed them. Public toilets, if they existed at all, were a rarity. Children defecated whenever and wherever the need arose. They wore baggy trousers with a split between the legs from just below the front waistband to the rear and didn't wear underwear. When nature called, they'd squat where they were, relying on the opening in their trousers to be adequate to allow safe passage of whatever they deposited. They had no need for toilet paper, the movement of their trousers performing the necessary wiping after the fact. Women held their little children out, squatting with legs apart, and whistled softly to encourage them to urinate in the gutters.

In spite of all this the Chinese were fastidious about their ablutions. In the early mornings they could be seen doing their stately, graceful, slow-motion exercises after which they'd wash themselves thoroughly, brush their teeth using a white powder to whiten them and scrape the 'fur' off their tongues with horseshoe shaped pieces of brass until they'd retch and vomit.

The streets of Peking were home for hundreds, perhaps thousands of beggars. They'd sit on the footpath calling for alms, or follow you down the street shaking their small tins that held a few copper coins pushing them forward to attract attention. Some of the beggars were horribly disfigured or disabled, and many had been deliberately incapacitated to help with their trade. Others appeared to beg from choice.

That was the Peking I remembered as a very small child.

CHAPTER 2

EARLY YEARS

Every seven years my parents were due for homeland furlough so when I was three we boarded the TSS *Tanda* (I was told the TSS stood for turbine steam ship) bound for Australia. I thought it was huge as it towered over us at its berth alongside the wharf. Its funnel seemed to be up in the sky and when its whistle sounded, I covered my ears, sure my head would burst with the noise.

Shortly after we were at sea a wrestling troupe entertained us with demonstrations on deck. There was also a magician and a group of jugglers but for me the real excitement came when we neared the Equator and King Neptune dressed in flowing robes with a bushy white beard and a skew-whiff crown on his head, hosted a feast in his own honour. The passengers joined in a variety of competitions; the part I liked best was when men in their pyjamas had pillow fights on the greasy pole over the swimming pool. The bouts usually ended with both contestants falling in. As the big moment arrived King Neptune called on all the children to be very quiet and listen for the bump as the ship crossed the equator. After the party we all waved goodbye as he climbed over the ship's rail to return to his home in Davy Jones' locker.

The trip to Australia seemed to take ages. On the way we stopped at places with interesting-sounding names like Rabaul and Thursday Island where little, naked, black boys paddled up to the ship in their tiny canoes and dived for the coins that we threw into the sea, retrieving them as they fluttered back and forth in the crystal-clear water.

It took three weeks to get to Sydney, where we steamed through the heads, then down the harbour towards the mighty bridge which had been built while my parents were away. We stood on the deck gazing upwards at the mass of steel, sure that the *Tanda's* mast couldn't possibly fit under it. We got closer and closer, then we were through and out the other side.

After a couple of days in Sydney the ship carried on down to Melbourne, where we disembarked to spend a few days before setting off for Colac, which was my folks' home town. It's on the Princes Highway just over ninety miles west of Melbourne. My recollections of Australia are pretty fragmented, we were there for only six months. I remember going to an exhibition at the Melbourne Exhibition Building. At a stand just inside the entrance, a man was demonstrating small coloured celluloid boomerangs with a launcher that sent them winging around the building and back to him. Another stand was promoting the new Ford V8 with a film show of Mickey Mouse as a magician creating the wonderful car. In the finale Mickey placed the V on the front of the radiator then took up a position in the centre of the V and dissolved into the number 8 which was the Ford V8 trademark. I also remember a very large parachute suspended inside the exhibition hall. However as I think back there may not have been a parachute there at all; it was probably the inside of the giant dome and I'd never seen anything like it before.

We spent most of the furlough time at Colac where we youngsters were a bit of a curiosity with the funny way we spoke. I remember being dressed up in my Chinese costume—a pale green silk waist coat, a pair of white trousers, black cloth shoes a small black skull cap with red button on top—and singing in Mandarin on the stage of the Victoria Hall. The audience were so delighted with my performance that they showered me with coins. Some weeks later I had to repeat my performance in the Melbourne Exhibition Building at a function to promote the work of missionaries in China. So that I could be seen on the stage, they stood me up on a chair where I sang a bracket of songs in Chinese. As I returned to my seat alongside my mother I'm told that I asked indignantly; 'Doesn't anybody pay here?' Mum was mortified as the lady sitting in front of us turned round and handed me a shiny silver threepenny bit.

During that six months I'd learnt all sorts of useful things about Australia. Songs like:

O How I wish that I could be
A little Aborigine.
He hunts and fishes all day long
And paddles in a billabong.

I'd no idea what a billabong was, and thought it was a kind of boat. Then there was:

Oh little baby bear
Has fur instead of hair,
And he lives in the top of a gum, gum, gum.
He climbs upstairs as fast
As a sailor up a mast,
Although he's as round as a drum, drum, drum.

But the song I liked best was a delicate little waltz that my sister learnt to play on the piano. I've not heard it since:

Over the plains with the emu,
That's where I'd just love to go,
Snuggled right down in his feathers,
Softer than most beds I know.
Wouldn't we go along quickly,
Almost as fast as a train,
But when it came to my bed time,
I'd want my mother again.

There are a few other memories that don't seem to fit into any sort of pattern: once getting bogged in the mud in the Tin Lizzie, a T-Model Ford, and being pulled out by powerful draught horses; on another occasion after the car got bogged, completing our journey through the mud on a sled pulled by huge Clydesdales; mushrooming in a paddock and being chased by my uncle's horse. My uncle was a bread carter and his horse Dodger, which was as quiet as a lamb, probably wandered over to help, we thought that he was after us and went for our lives. I tore my jumper on the lower strand of the barbed-wire fence as I scrambled under it. Another delicious memory is of lying on the bed in the sleep-out listening to the rain beating down on the corrugated iron roof—we only had tiled roofs in China. And the thunder! I'd never heard anything like it before. I thought it was a Chinese man up there banging a drum. I recall walks through the park down near the lake where there were kangaroos, emus and rabbits; being stung by a bull ant; the little pink rabbit slippers that I got for Christmas and sitting on an upturned pail near the cow bail, watching my uncle milk the cow. Then it was time to go back China.

We were given quite a send-off by friends, relations and a large contingent of Salvation Army officers, and as we boarded the *Tanda* once again we were presented with a boomerang that had a kookaburra, kangaroo and a map of Australia burnt into it and the words Taroona Yuntha—'you will come back'.

On the return voyage we called at Tokyo, then visited Yokohama where we saw Fujiama. My recollections of Japan are scant apart from a wind-up toy car that my parents bought me. The fascinating little thing wouldn't run off the table top, when it got to the edge it just turned and went off in another direction.

When we returned to China, we went back to Peking. It was winter and fearfully cold. The Chinese peasants were wearing grey quilted jackets and trousers, padded caps with flaps that covered their ears and could be tied under the chin and heavy cloth mittens. Snow covered everything, lying in deep drifts against walls and weighing down tree branches until they cracked under their load. Icicles hung from the eaves of houses while the lakes and rivers froze over. We wore thick padded clothes with fur hats, gloves and ear-muffs to protect us from the biting chill of the north winds that howled in from Mongolia.

This time we moved into a house in the compound at the rear of the Salvation Army's Territorial Headquarters in Morrison Street. Our servants from Ping Arn Farng joined us and moved into the servants' quarters which were in a separate enclosure off the main compound. Several missionary families lived in the compound in two storeyed grey brick houses that were far more modern than Ping Arn Farng. They had electricity and running water and, best of all, central heating from a coal-burning furnace in the basement *and* they had casement windows with glass in them. Over the bath there was an upright white metal cylinder which was a gas-burning water heater; we called it a geyser and pronounced it geezer. It was a temperamental creature which was viewed with suspicion by my mother and with terror by the amah because of its propensity for

22

'blowing up'. On its front was an aperture behind which was the gas ring. Extending across this aperture were a couple of chrome levers that regulated the beast's gas and water flow. On Saturday night, which was bath night, Dad or, if he was away, and he frequently was, Mum lit the geyser with trepidation. We all stayed clear of the bathroom while it was gurgling away, just in case.

In the yard we youngsters made a small ice-skating rink by dividing off a portion of the garden with an earth wall about four or five inches high and then hosing the enclosure each day. After a few days there was a layer of ice strong enough to support our weight as we learned how to skate on ice skates that we'd bought from a second hand stall. When we'd become more proficient we were allowed to go to Pei Hai Park where a section of the frozen lake had been fenced off with woven bamboo matting to form a public rink. A few cents admission gave us the chance to mingle with the experts; brilliant figure skaters, speed skaters and elderly gentlemen carrying out the graceful actions of their t'ai chi exercises on ice skates. We were always attended by one of our servants, for occasionally a bit of excitement would be added when the brave or foolhardy skated outside the enclosure and fell through thin ice into the freezing waters of the lake.

Not long after we'd settled back into life in Peking, I was taken to hospital because some yellow scabs had formed on the end of my 'thing'. The nurses took my clothes from me and dressed me in a white gown before putting me in a cot. Although I was standing up I couldn't see over the top rail and cried as, through the bars, I watched my family walk away leaving me with strangers. Next morning I was taken to the operating theatre where the doctor placed a horrible smelling metal and gauze mask over my nose and mouth. When I woke I saw that my penis had a fat bandage around it and it hurt so much that I cried when I did wee wees. I didn't know it then, but I had just been circumcised.

With spring came the thaw and, as only the major roads of Peking were sealed, the grey/black slush of muddy unmade roads. But as the days lengthened the trees came into bud and the birds returned, the bitter winds eased around to the south, the sun shone and daffodils coloured the gardens. North China had four distinct seasons so we could pack away our padded winter clothes and fleecy-lined underwear, knowing we wouldn't need them again until the end of autumn.

In the lovely spring days our family and some of our missionary friends would set off in our rickshaws to visit the Summer Palace with its picturesque gardens and lakes with humpbacked and zigzag bridges built to foil the progress of evil spirits. The Chinese have a healthy respect for evil spirits. Buildings are erected to give maximum protection from them. Lions and dragons adorn roof ridges and each row of roofing tiles finishes with a lion or dragon face. In spite of the ubiquitous nature of spirits they have one common characteristic that renders them susceptible to trickery; they only travel in straight lines, they cannot turn corners! So an evil spirit can't negotiate a zig zag bridge. A hump backed bridge across a stream will deflect a spirit skywards. The roofs of houses have an upward kick at the eaves so any evil spirit dropping from the sky, will get deflected upwards as it slides down the roof and be shot back into space. At floor level across the doorway of house entrances is a large piece of wood about a foot or fifteen inches high and a couple of inches thick. Any spirit scuttling along the ground, intent on gaining entry, hits this and is bounced back whence it came.

Evil spirits, dragons and gods played a big part in Chinese everyday life. With his picture stuck on the back of the kitchen door the Kitchen God was in a position to take note of pretty well everything that went on in a household. I never got the impression he was a terribly affable fellow as he glowered down at me, but the servants didn't seem to mind him and once a year on his feast day, they'd peel down his picture and burn it on a funeral pyre in the yard, together with paper replicas of food and cakes and all sorts of other things like horses and carts and consumer goods that could be of use to him in the spirit world. There'd be burning of incense and letting off of firecrackers and skyrockets. Everyone had a grand time. Next morning they'd go down to a market stall and buy another Kitchen God to be pasted in his place of honour behind the kitchen door.

A similar procedure was gone through at burials. Wealthy Chinese had huge funeral processions led by the professional mourners who'd been keening at the residence of the deceased for the days leading up to the interment. Following the mourners came people bearing lifesized coloured paper and bamboo reproductions of all that might possibly be required to make things comfortable for the deceased in the next life. In the parade were men blowing long trumpets much like alpine horns which made a deep 'oo-oooo, oo-oooo' sound. These, along with copious quantities of firecrackers were designed to frighten away evil spirits. Finally came the coffin in an enormous hearse the size of a small room. A grand affair, it was set on carrying poles and borne along by thirty or forty bearers. Built to look like a traditional Chinese house, it was painted red and gold, with pitched roof and ornate decorations of lions' heads and dragons. At the place of burial all the paper goodies would be burnt, together with silver-paper money and incense to help the deceased on his journey to the afterlife. When the chap from down the road died, he lay in state in the front room of his house for a month while professional mourners wailed day and night at the his door. As friends of the family we were all invited to witness the sealing of the coffin—I think we were the only Foreigners there. A huge feast had been prepared and our erstwhile neighbour smiled at us beatifically, if somewhat inscrutably, from his place of honour amongst the folds of white silk that adorned his coffin. Somehow I don't think the embalmers had done much of a job. It was mid-summer and the stench was unbelievable. We could barely breathe in the room much less partake of the sumptuous repast, but the other guests did not appear to share our discomfort.

We were taught that the lunar eclipse was caused when the Earth got in the way and cast its shadow across the moon but the Chinese weren't fooled. They knew that the eclipse was caused when a hungry dragon in the sky swallowed the moon. To frighten the dragon away, they'd let off crackers and rockets; crash gongs and cymbals and beat drums. It was noisy, but it worked. Eventually the dragon, taking fright, would regurgitate the moon and take flight. Firecrackers were a part of life, they were used at every excuse and frequently when no excuse was needed. Describing them the Chinese said the big ones, the double bangers went 'ger bung' whereas the little ones tied together in strings went 'pilapalapilapalapilapala-poooong'—the pooooong was the big one at the end.

Back to the Summer Palace. The zigzag bridges may have been daunting for devils but we thought them fun. Another favourite place was the Marble Boat. All shining white and flashing in the sun, it was as large as a three-storey house. We were fascinated by its story. Although now it operated as a tea-house it had originally been built by the Empress Dowager for her own pleasure. It seems her advisers had tried to impress upon her the need for a navy to protect China from invasion. Instead, the noble lady spent the funds set aside for the project on the construction of the marble boat which was sited beside the lake in her Summer Palace.

Once the ice had melted, Pei Hai Park became a popular picnic spot and the lake was covered with rowing boats. We'd often go there for picnics on hot summer days. In the evenings, especially during the lantern festival, the park would be ablaze with colour as trees were decked with paper lanterns of all shapes and sizes, and dragon boats— long rowing boats with their prows carved like dragons' heads and adorned with lanterns—glided across the glistening waters of the lake.

Sometimes we'd visit the Temple of Heaven and the Altar of Heaven and on rare occasions we'd be allowed admission to the Forbidden City which held the treasures of dynasties of emperors, the very old motor cars, the priceless tapestries and embroideries and exquisite jade carvings.

As spring gave way to summer, stifling hot winds brought red dust storms from the Gobi Desert that reduced visibility to a few feet. When we were out of doors we'd wear topees—pith helmets— to protect our heads and the backs of our necks against sunstroke and we often had to breathe through gauze masks or handkerchiefs to keep out the choking dust. To provide some respite from the heat most of the Salvation Army missionary families spent the summer holidays at the Western Hills in a large rambling two storeyed rest house which had a wide verandah around the outside and was set in extensive park like gardens. Some days 'donkey boys' would hire us almost somnolent donkeys and mules to take us on rides through the hills to secluded picnic spots. Of course we always took our servants so that they could prepare our meals and 'do for us'. They'd bring along the ice cream churn, a barrel like contraption with an internal metal container with a crank handle. Inside the metal container was the ice cream mixture and packed around the container was crushed ice laced with salt to stop it from melting. When we reached our destination one of the servants would wind the handle for half an hour or so which churned the ice cream mix until it solidified.

Tennis was a favourite pastime and I learnt to play at a very early age with an old wooden racket that was flat on the top and looked like a snow shoe. It had to be kept in a press which had failed sadly in its attempt to stop the racket from warping. For practice my brother and I spent much of our time hitting a ball against a brick wall. We played on the courts at the rest house early in the morning or in the cool of the evening—when we were in Peking, we played on courts in the Union Church grounds. The Union Church was an ecumenical arrangement whereby the non-conformist denominations of the Christian Church combined for united worship. The conduct of the services was rotated amongst the various groups with the service being led by a minister from one denomination and the sermon preached by a minister from another. The system worked well. It wasn't until we came to Australia to live that I found, to my amazement, that the Church was divided up into denominations with differing dogmas.

The Chinese kids, the Chinks as we called them, didn't play the sorts of games we played, though they were very good at hopscotch and marbles, but had different rules to us. They were also very keen on soccer and spent a lot of time practising their footwork with a tennis balls, but mainly they had their own games. They made a kind of shuttlecock by tying a couple of chicken feathers to a small bronze 'cash'—those Chinese bronze coins with the square hole cut in the middle. The aim of the game was to see how long they could keep the shuttlecock from touching the ground by kicking it into the air with the side of the foot. Good players could keep the thing going for a quarter of an hour at a time and performed all manner of acrobatic actions as they did so.

Another popular pastime was spinning a kind of whistling top that was shaped like a dumbbell and spun by balancing it on a string between two sticks. With a stick in each hand, the player would keep the top spinning by whipping it with the string and tossing it into the air. Flutes cut in the sides of the top made it whistle with a rising and falling siren sound as its speed fluctuated. It looked easy enough but I never mastered the technique. The Chinese were fond of whistles, they'd tie tiny flutes to the wings of homing pigeons so they'd whistle as they flew overhead, and keep whistling crickets in small bamboo cages. They were also fond of songbirds. Old men often walked around the streets with bamboo cages that contained their pet thrushes or larks.

Towards the end of the year my father was transferred to Shanghai. Our belongings were packed into metal trunks that were locked then bound tightly with wet straw rope. The ropes would shrink as they dried and had to be cut to open the trunks. It was an effective method of protection against minor pilferage The train journey took a couple of days and on our arrival we moved into no. 8, a four-storey house at the end of Yang Terrace off Wei Hai Wei Road. We were just around the corner from Yates Road which ran into Nanking Road, an extension of Bubbling Well Road, one of Shanghai's major thoroughfares. Bubbling Well Road was named after a rather dirty well that was fenced off by the roadside, it was pretty putrid and was probably a cesspool but I used to enjoy gazing down into it, watching the black bubbles rising up and bursting at the surface with a soft plop. All the main roads of the city were clogged with handcarts, wheelbarrows and rickshaws which had to compete for space with cars, trams, buses and electrically operated trolley-buses. With no consideration for the traffic, pedestrians meandered without control all over the carriageway. Nanking Road seemed to be a constant traffic jam with the deafening din of car horns, tram bells, shouting rickshaw coolies and the incessant squeal of barrow wheels. It was where the large multi-storeyed department stores of Wing On and Sinceres were situated.

Unlike Peking, Shanghai was a major city, very much part of the twentieth century and although it was on the Chinese mainland it was, like Hong Kong, not really part of China. The city was divided into concessions. The French concession was very French, with gendarmes patrolling streets with names like Ave Foche and Ave Petain, whereas the British concession was 'friflly' British with turbaned Sikh policemen on point duty at the intersections and a huge Union Jack painted on the road to indicate where the concession started. Then there was the International Settlement which was a law unto itself. China was a violent place. Walking down the street one day my mother was attracted by a commotion at a street corner. She pressed through the crowd curious to see what was causing the disturbance and found to her horror a street side execution was about to take place. Unable to push her way back through the crowd she watched as the culprits, their hands tied behind their backs, were led down the road before being forced to kneel at the curb-side. The executioner, a burly fellow, stepped forward deftly wielding a gigantic sword with which he effortlessly beheaded the hapless felons. Their heads were placed on stakes and left at the street corner as a deterrent to other evil doers.

Captain and Mrs Dempster were American Salvation Army officers who had been in language school with my parents, and were stationed at a small hospital in the country. They had three children, a daughter and two sons. One morning a gang of bandits from the nearby hills forced their way into the captain's office, demanding money from the safe. He didn't act promptly enough so they shot him dead. Their youngest child, who was four, was in the room at the time. Determined not to depart empty handed, the bandits demanded Mrs Dempster give them her gold wedding ring, threatening to cut off her finger if she did not hand it over.

After the tragedy, Mrs Dempster elected to stay on in China with the children so she was appointed to Shanghai where there were other officers to give the family support. The youngest Dempster was about my age. As we played together he'd often say over and over, 'Bad man shoot my Daddy. Bang bang Daddy dead.'

At that time Shanghai was reckoned to be the fourth largest city in the world and had the second worst crime rate just pipped at the post by Chicago. Police patrolled the streets in Red Marias—large, fire-engine-coloured armoured, riot-breaking vehicles the size of furniture vans with shiny brass machine-guns mounted on top. The news caster for Shanghai's Radio Station XMHA was Carol Alcott, who wore a bulletproof vest when out on his rounds. He used to start his broadcasts with, 'Hello, hello, hello, this is Carol Alcott speaking from Radio XMHA Shanghai'. Later he started to advertise Jello so he changed his opening line to, 'Jello, jello, jello, this is Carol Alcott . . .'

Shanghai's streets were crowded with beggars. At night it was impossible to walk on the footpath for sleeping forms. Whenever rice was unloaded at shops, beggars stood around with cracked bowls or empty cans, brushing into them the surplus grains off the outside of the bags. Although poverty was rife, with pickpockets and petty criminals abounding, none of that seemed to be of too much concern to me. Yang Terrace was in a compound set behind a high brick wall with access through a large gate that was guarded by the gatekeeper. From the gate a tar-sealed road ran in front of the houses. The rear of the houses was serviced by a concrete path, along which large brick rubbish bins were built where we hid when we played hide and seek. On the other side of the sealed road each house had a fenced private garden. There were eight houses in our terrace. The ground floor of our place comprised the kitchen, servants' quarters and storeroom. On the first floor we had the sitting room and a dining room that opened out onto an enclosed veranda. Our bedrooms were on the third floor, and on the fourth floor we had our playroom which also housed the large cistern to ensure adequate water pressure for the house. Like most houses in Shanghai our place was centrally heated from a large coal-burning furnace in the cellar, with pipes that channelled hot water to the heater units throughout the rooms of the house.

We had a cook, an amah, and a rickshaw coolie who doubled as yardman. Each Monday my father had a meeting with the cook to establish the week's menu, after which the cook would arrange everything from the purchasing of the foodstuffs to the preparation and serving of the meals. Apart from looking after us, the amah was responsible for the general housework, the washing, the ironing and the mending. Each morning she'd come to my bedroom and lay out my clothes, then help me dress. After I'd gone down to breakfast she'd make my bed and tidy up my room.

My father's office was down near the Bund, which was pronounced as it's spelt, not 'boond' as seems to be the modern affectation. Along the Bund were strings of godowns enormous storage warehouses near the wharves which held the cargoes from the ships that sailed up the Wang Poo, (the Yellow River), to service the port of Shanghai. From the Bund tiny sampans and great lumbering junks shuttled across to Pootung on the other side of the river. As well as being a busy thoroughfare, the river served as a dump for the city's refuse. Bobbing amongst the rubbish that swirled and eddied around the pylons of the great wharves were the swollen putrid bodies of dead cats, dogs and pigs or, occasionally, even people.

Anything that you couldn't get from the door to door hawkers you could buy at Wing On's, which was a large multi storeyed department store, where we did most our shopping. Of course the attendants were all Chinese, Foreigners didn't do that sort of work. That's where my father took me, to the barber's shop on the ground floor, for my first hair cut. The walls were covered with mirrors so that when you sat in the barber's chair you could see your reflection and the reflection of your reflection and the reflection of the reflection of your reflection on and on and on, and you got smaller and smaller the further you went, but you kept on going and getting smaller, going on and on and it never, never ended. I remember crying when the clippers pulled as the Chinese barber set to work, but not as much as my mother cried when she saw that my golden curls were gone forever.

On most Saturdays our family went to the racecourse. It was right in the centre of the city and Shanghai's major sports ground. While the ponies raced around the perimeter, the area in the middle was used for other activities such as polo, tennis and baseball. There was even a small nine-hole golf course where my father sometimes tested his skill with a mashie, niblick or spoon. The American Marines ran a baseball competition with the Marines' band supplying the musical entertainment. During those 'tween war' years the popular music scene was going through a curious phase. The hits of the time were songs like 'A-tisket a-tasket I lost my yellow basket' or:

Down in the meadow in the Itchi Pitchi Poo
Swam three little fishes and a Mama fishy too.
'Swim,' said the Mama Fishy, 'swim if you can.'
So they swam and they swam right over the dam.
Boomps boomps diddum doddum waddem choo . . .

Another favourite was the 'Donkey Serenade'.

The band played these masterpieces during the ball games, and wherever possible matched the songs to the activity that took place down on the diamond; if a batter was struck out we'd get 'Boo hoo, I'll tell my mother on you, boo hoo'.

It was at this time that a huge neon sign of an enormous hive with coloured bees flying around it, was erected to advertise Beehive knitting wool. It was claimed to be the largest neon sign in the world, and at night we could see it from our attic windows at Yang Terrace.

The Da Lo swimming pool was built at that time too, and we went along to the official opening. It was a gigantic place with several smaller pools off the main one and fountains and springboards and a thirty foot diving tower and large horns on poles that blared out the latest in popular music. It had a snack bar where you could buy Eskimo Pies—ice creams coated in dark chocolate—or popcorn and Green Spot—a delicious orangeade. It probably also catered for more sophisticated tastes but I didn't understand about such things. We became members at the Da Lo, and that's where I learnt to swim.

My brother and I built a hand cart which we used as our first money-making venture, pulling the kids around Yang Terrace for five cents a ride. We did pretty well on our first day in business but our entrepreneurial skills were short-lived. When our parents learnt the source of our new-found wealth they made us return our hard-earned cash. However, we found other ways to entertain ourselves. We built a swing between a couple of trees which was great fun; after grazing copious quantities of skin from knees and elbows, I learnt to ride a bike; sometimes we'd ring the doorbells of the other houses in the terrace, then run and hide; or when our neighbours had visitors who arrived in motor cars, if we caught the chauffeur in an inattentive moment, we'd creep up and wedge a match into a tyre valve to let out the air.

My father had a RCA Victor gramophone of which he was very proud. It stood in the corner of the first-floor verandah in its own large cabinet with records stored in a cupboard underneath it. You had to wind it up with a handle and change needles after every record. The small shiny steel needles came in a little tin with a picture of a dog listening to a gramophone horn on its lid. For a while we tried bamboo needles which could be resharpened, but they weren't much of a success. My mothers favourite record was the intermezzo from *Cavaleria Rusticana*, but mine was a song, 'Cuckoo, cuckoo it comes from the cuckoo clock'. When I was home on my own I'd open the verandah windows so the birds in the trees outside could hear while I played the record for them.

On Sundays we'd go to Sunday school at the Anglican Cathedral. One afternoon my brother had permission to visit a friend on his way home. It was getting late and my parents were becoming uneasy when the telephone rang—strangely I still remember our phone number, it was 34063—it was the Shanghai Police Chief, a very pukka Englishman, wanting to speak to my father.

'Major Begley do you have a son Ian?'

Yes my father did.

'We've got him here at the police station. He's just shot a Chinaman.'

Dad rushed to Police Headquarters and was shown into an interrogation room where a very nervous lad awaited his arrival.

It appears that he and his friend were doing some target practice with an air rifle, shooting at a tree outside the first-floor window. The gun had inadvertently discharged hitting a Chinese gentleman in the corner of the eye. Fortunately the eye was not damaged but, as luck would have it, the victim, happened to be the less than popular land-lord of the house where the friend lived. The police were called, a complaint lodged and my brother, who was handling the rifle at the time was taken into custody, to 'put the fear of God into him'. I need hardly say that my father was unimpressed with his eldest son's behaviour, but accidents do happen and no serious damage had been done.

Years later, when we were adults, my father was recounting the incident when my brother confessed, 'I suppose I'm old enough now to tell you it wasn't an accident. I'd taken a pot shot at the bloke'.

CHAPTER 3

LONG LIVE THE KING!

The Durham Light Infantry was stationed in Shanghai and used to put on grand displays of trooping the colour at the racecourse. Sometimes at night they'd beat the tattoo with a magnificent performance of Tchaikovsky's '1812 Overture', complete with cannon blasts from their field guns. It was spectacular but rather terrifying. When King George V died, they put on a lavish display to demonstrate their allegiance to the new monarch. As youngsters our imaginations were captured by the drama of the doctor watching by the Royal bedside. Fingers on faltering pulse he waited, sensitive to the faintest flicker of the failing heart. Then, when the inevitable moment came, he announced: 'The King is dead, long live the King'.

We had a new king, Edward VIII! It was exciting stuff, but then something went wrong. I didn't understand what, but we little boys were soon singing a ditty:

Who's that walking down the aisle,
Mrs Simpson with a smile,
Holding onto Eddie's prick
Thinking it's his walking stick.

I wasn't sure who Eddie was and I'd never heard of Mrs Simpson. After the abdication came the coronation and it was King George VI and Queen Elizabeth that everyone was cheering. A holiday was declared and we had sports at the racecourse where we were given coronation medals which had been struck with pictures of the new King and Queen. We stood to attention to sing 'God save the King' and I covered my ears when the twenty one field guns gave the royal salute, sending puffs of grey/white smoke drifting across the sky.

When I was old enough to start school, I was kitted out with a uniform and sent off in a bus with my sister to be enrolled in Shanghai's Cathedral School for Girls. Little boys went to the girls' school for their first few years until they were old enough to transfer over to the prep school of the Cathedral School for Boys which had been originally set up by an endowment to educate the choir boys of the Anglican Holy Trinity Cathedral. The Cathedral School uniform included a purple blazer with the school crest on the pocket. The crest was made up of the Union Jack, a rampant lion on a blue background and three golden lions on a red background. The girls' school crest had the Union Jack hanging vertically while on the boys' school crest it was horizontal across the top. The schools were both very proper and very British as were all the students. The teachers were all English and the curriculum was laid down by Cambridge University. On my parents' salary it would have been impossible to afford the fees, but the Dean of the Cathedral kindly waived the fees on the understanding that my brother and I would join the choir when a vacancy occurred. I was put into a class called 'transition' which was designed to get children used to the ways of school. The rooms seemed to me to be very big, with long church-type windows, pointed at the top, that stretched from the ceiling down to a sloping window ledge just above desk level. Through the windows you could look out across the spacious grounds where clumps of yellow daffodils nodded and swayed in swathes of green. I longed to go out there to play.

During recess on my first day I saw a boy in my class burying some small live frogs in a pile of earth. I had an almost obsessive love for animals, birds and insects so I pushed him aside and frantically started digging to rescue the tiny creatures while some of the girls ran in to tell the teacher who, when she saw me digging, assumed me to be the guilty party. My protestations of innocence were to no avail. I was reprimanded in front of the class for being a horrible, cruel little boy and kept in during the lunch break. School wasn't the sort of place I really wanted to be.

China and Japan had been at war for some time and the fighting was starting to affect our lives in Shanghai. Refugees by the thousands streamed into the city, adding to the enormous number of beggars who cluttered the streets. The Salvation Army set up refugee camps and food kitchens to house and feed as many as they could, but the numbers were overwhelming. Unwanted newborn baby girls were sometimes left on the rubbish dumps that were on most street corners and all vacant areas of land. Whenever we found them, during our wanderings about the city, we'd tell our parents who'd arrange for the babies to be taken to one of the many homes that had been set up to care for them.

The outer suburb of Hongku was a kind of no-man's land where sporadic hand-to-hand combat took place. Although it was strictly out of bounds, on the way home from school, we sometimes went there looking for war souvenirs. We'd find all sorts of interesting things like bullets or pieces of shrapnel. During one of these forays, one of the older boys, who was more adventurous than the rest of us, led us further into no-man's-land than we'd ever gone before. We'd collected several bits of shrapnel and a few spent bullet casings when he picked up a hand grenade, pulled the pin and threw it as far as he could. We waited with our hands over our ears, but when nothing happened he ran over and picked it up to see what had gone wrong. A second later it exploded blowing off his right hand and blinding him in one eye.

In panic, the rest of us turned to run but he called out, 'We're scouts we've got to stick together. Quick, go and get help.'

After they got him to hospital the doctors stitched up the stump of his right arm, patched his eye socket and removed lumps of shrapnel from his cheek and his shin. It was a long time before we ventured back to Hongku.

The Japanese made frequent night bombing raids on Shanghai's gasometers, so the city was blacked out at night. Heavy curtains had to cover any windows if lights were on indoors. Inspectors patrolled the streets and if the slightest chink of light could be seen from outside you ran the risk of severe fines. Cars headlights were covered so that only the tiniest slit of light shone through. To protect from flying glass in the event of explosions close by, we cut strips of paper and glued them in a crisscross pattern to all the windowpanes at Yang Terrace. In the evenings when the air-raid sirens sounded, we'd switch off all the house lights so we could watch from the attic windows as the flights of dive bombers manoeuvred to keep out of the stabbing rays of the search lights. A plane would detach itself from the main group, wheel to dodge the exploding anti-aircraft shells, then plunge in a power dive with sirens howling, pulling out at the last moment to climb to the safety of the night sky. Seconds later we'd hear the thud of the exploding bombs. Fortunately for us the bombing missions were never successful. Not only would a direct hit have cut off Shanghai's gas supply, but it was believed the resultant explosion could have devastated the city.

Dog fights often took place over the city in daylight and much to our mother's horror, my brother and I would run around picking up the spent bullets as they fell to the ground. During one such dog-fight, some Japanese fighters attacked a Chinese dive bomber. To lighten his load the Chinese pilot jettisoned his bombs aiming them at the racecourse. His aim was not as good as his intentions and the bombs landed in the central business district doing a lot of damage to property and killing scores of his countrymen.

Eventually the authorities decided that Shanghai was no place for us, so a truce was declared to give time for all Foreign women and children to be evacuated; the menfolk were to remain. At short notice we were told to prepare to be taken to Hong Kong. About 1300 of us assembled at the Bund where we were loaded onto lighters which ferried across to an ocean liner that stood by waiting for us at Pootung on the other side of the Hwang Poo. Just as we were about to board the ship the Japs broke the truce raking the decks with machine gun fire. Sailors leapt into action picking us up and throwing us bodily on board then down into the safety of the holds. As soon as we were aboard the ship ran the gauntlet of gunfire, steaming for the open sea as machine guns rattled and shells whined overhead.

Conditions below decks were crowded, as the ship had not been designed to accommodate such a large number of people. There weren't enough bunks to go round so we had to make ourselves as comfortable as possible in the confined space. Food rations were scant and I suppose the tempers of the adults started to wear pretty thin in the couple of days it took to get us to Hong Kong. On our arrival we were accommodated in a multi-storeyed block of flats at Kowloon. Our flat was cramped but we did have a small verandah with a pot-plant where a praying mantis lived, and a roof garden where we could play. For some reason my sister had not come with us so I was sent along on my own to the Diocesan Girls' School. After school my brother and I often went to the YMCA where we swam in a heated indoor swimming pool. In those days you had to swim in the nuddy at all YMCAs. Life in Hong Kong was pleasant. The shops stocked marvellous things like Schuco toys and Dick cap guns, items that you couldn't get in North China, and everything was so cheap!

We'd only been there a few days when it started to rain, lightly at first, then building to a heavy downpour. That evening a lady from an adjoining flat knocked on our door to say there was a typhoon warning and we should put up our typhoon bars and batten down for the night. As we had no idea what a typhoon bar was she helped us locate them—solid oaken planks about five by two inches that attached to brackets inside the windows and external doors to stop them from being blown in by the wind. When she was satisfied that we were sufficiently secured she left us to sit and wait.

The rain built up into a torrent and soon the wind started to blow. It howled around the building, shaking the doors and rattling the glass as a fearful gale raged outside. The windows and French doors bowed and creaked against the typhoon bars as fountains of water burst through cracks in the walls. At the height of the storm the power failed. We huddled together fearfully in the darkness, wondering what the night had in store. Momentarily the room would flood with blue flame as bolts of lightening rent the sky. The crashes of thunder were drowned by the howling wind. But you can't sustain fear for long and eventually we slept. In the morning, when we woke to sunshine, the flat was a mess, there was water everywhere. Our doors and window casements, swollen by the rain water, were jammed tight, however the only real damage we sustained was when my brother broke the glass trying to open a window.

Outside it looked a bit like a war zone with large, uprooted trees lying strewn across the roads. A cargo ship moored at the dockside had been lifted by the mountainous seas to be deposited on the wharf. On the verandah apart from the mess of blown leaves, everything was all right. The pot-plant had been knocked over but the praying mantis was still there.

A few months later when the war scene in Shanghai had calmed sufficiently, we found ourselves aboard another ship setting off for home again. Sitting on the forward hold in brilliant sunshine my brother sang me a little song he'd learnt at school in Hong Kong. He explained that it was a lullaby sung by a mother to her baby whose father was away at sea:

Sweet and low, sweet and low,
Wind of the western sea.
Low, low, breathe and blow,
Wind of the western sea!
Over the rolling waters go,
Come from the dying moon, and blow,
Blow him again to me,
While my little one, while my pretty one, sleeps.

Sleep and rest, sleep and rest,
Father will come to thee soon;
Rest, rest on mother's breast,
Father will come to thee soon;
Father will come to his babe in the nest,
Silver sails all out of the west,
Under the silver moon.
Sleep my little one, sleep, my pretty one, sleep.

And I can still see, there, way out across to the horizon, a tiny boat with its silver sail set, coming out of the western horizon.

Shanghai had scarcely changed, the place still teemed with beggars and rickshaw coolies still followed you as you walked down the street, trying to persuade you to use their services. Of course at Yang Terrace we had our own rickshaw boy and other rickshaws were not allowed past the terrace gates, but whenever we walked out into Yates Road we'd be surrounded by beggars and followed by streams of rickshaw coolies calling and jostling for our attention. There was one major change however rickshaws were slowly being replaced by pedi-cabs—rickshaws that had the front part of a bicycle added to them in place of the shafts, so you now had a chap pedalling the thing along like a push bike.

But by now we'd learnt to ride bikes and apart from the ban on visiting Hongku, we were free to cycle all over the city, where we'd scoot about dodging around rickshaws and handcarts, trams, buses, cars and trolley-buses and the hordes of pedestrians who wandered randomly across the streets. Most of the major intersections were controlled by traffic lights operated by a policemen on point duty. In the centre of each intersection was a small round shelter where the policeman stood. He controlled the lights by means of a stick suspended between two ropes that were attached to an overhead switch. On the roof of each shelter there was invariably a stack of rickshaw seat cushions which had been confiscated by the policeman for misdemeanours or traffic infringements by the rickshaw boys. A group of shouting jostling rickshaw coolies gathered around the policemen's shelter pleading for return of the cushions without which it was impossible to attract a fare. In the British concession we soon got to be known by the Sikh policemen so when they saw us pedalling furiously down the road—we were always in a mad rush to get somewhere—they'd change the lights to green to let us through, giving us a smile and a wave.

By Shanghai standards we were far from well-off for Foreigners. I can't remember us ever having more than five servants and our parents certainly weren't flush with cash, not like the parents of the other kids at school who were doctors or lawyers or company directors of huge corporations like Jardine's, Swire's, the Blue Funnel Line or the Hong Kong and Shanghai Bank. These people lived in enormous mansions set in vast grounds tendered by an army of servants. They got around the city in chauffeur-driven Lincoln Zephyrs with musical horns and threw lavish parties to which we were sometimes invited and showered with expensive presents. My brother and I went to one such Christmas party in our rickshaw which had a removable waterproof canopy to protect us from the elements. We alighted at the imposing gates of the compound and were ushered through several moon gates—circular gateways in the internal walls of the compound—into an inner courtyard where the mansion stood ablaze with light and lavishly festooned with Christmas decorations. Inside, the house was a riot of colour and music with holly and ivy and joyous Christmas carols. Hanging from a chandelier in the ballroom was an immense bunch of mistletoe which we little boys carefully avoided lest we be subjected to the indignity of being kissed. It was a wonderful party with all kinds of food and sweets and delicacies. Indeed it was there that I saw Santa

Claus, with his sleigh and team of fleet-footed reindeer, sweeping down from the sky to land in a cloud of snow.

It was about seven o'clock and outside the snow fell steadily when suddenly a shout went up, 'Here comes Santa Claus'.

'Where, where?' we all asked.

'Out there. Up in the sky.'

We crowded to the windows brushing away the frost and condensation from the glass with our hands. It was dark out there. Snowflakes swirled passed the window like flashing white sparks and I could see long silver icicles hanging from the eaves.

'I can't see anything'. I cried.

'Yes you can, look up. There he is, see the reindeers and the sleigh. There, he's coming down to land on the lawn! See him!'

And I did. I saw them, the graceful reindeer with their legs bent in flight, the sleigh, with the man in the red suit, arching down from the sky to land a small distance away in a cloud of powdered snow.

I knew it was Santa Claus because a few moments later there was a rap on the front door, which burst open to reveal him in his bright red suit with his black boots, his flowing white hair and beard. Flakes of snow sparkled on his hat and on the huge sack he carried over his right shoulder that was filled to bursting with a wondrous array of toys.

Often since I've decked myself out in a red costume with a white wig, and handed out presents to children at parties, or elderly folk in hospitals, but . . . well, that's only pretending.

I graduated to the Prep School of the Cathedral School for Boys where there were more 'boy type' things to keep me occupied. I joined the Cubs and the Shanghai Society for the Prevention of Cruelty to Animals. Periodically the people from the SSPCA would visit the school bringing with them an enormous Galapagos tortoise which lumbered slowly around the lawns with long neck outstretched, and 'Old Soldier'—a horse which had been decorated in the Great War. They taught us how to treat and handle horses, and about fetlocks and frogs and withers.

It was around this time that my brother and I joined the Anglican Holy Trinity Cathedral Choir. We dressed in black cassocks with white surplices, high starched collars and purple bow ties and were paid $2 for attending rehearsals, $2 for Sunday services and $4 for weddings. At that time, as I recall, there were about twelve Shanghai dollars to the Australian pound so our pay was a great source of pocket money. The choir stalls were so high I had to stand up on the kneeling pad to see over the top when the choir was singing. During the rest of the service we either watched the squeaking bats as they flew above us, fluttering in and out of the belfry and the organ loft, or else we went to sleep. The head chorister would pass a nudge down the line when we had to do our next bit of singing.

Religion was somewhat of a mystery to me, it was full of quaint rituals that I could not understand. Curious things like the Magnificat and the Apostles Creed and all sorts of Chants, none of which I understood, but gifted with a good memory, I learnt them all and sang my part.

It wasn't only the church services that confused me, at home during family prayers we'd sing:

Jesus bids us shine with a clear pure light
Like a little candle burning in the night.

I thought the words were 'like a little camel burning in the night' and had a mental image of a small camel with a flame coming out of the top of its hump. I thought it was nice. When it came time to pray we'd recite:

Gentle Jesus meek and mild
Look upon a little child
Pity my simplicity . . .

Now that really had me guessing, because that last line came across to me as:

'Pity mice in plicity'. I had no idea what a 'plicity' was, but it must be a dreadful place and if those poor little mice had got themselves in there, I was sure they needed all the pity they could get.

I came home one afternoon to find the house deserted. Of course the servants were there, but on every floor it was the same, all the rooms were deserted. I sat down on the back stairs and cried and cried and cried. At last, after what seemed like hours to me, my mother came home. She observed as she comforted me that I had a fever, so a doctor was sent for. His examination led to the conclusion that I must be quarantined at once as I had German measles. This, he decided, was the cause of my acute distress. Well, he might have been right about the German measles, but he was very wrong about the distress. I had learnt in Sunday School that on that 'Great Day' when the last trumpet sounded, the 'good'—God's chosen—would be swept up to be with their Lord. The evil doers, however, would be left behind. 'Two people would be in a field', the Sunday School teacher had said, 'one would be taken, the other left. Two would be together in a bed, one would be taken, the other left.' I knew that despite my best endeavours, there were many, many times when I was far from being a 'good boy', and that afternoon I was sure that the rest of the family had been swept up into the clouds to claim their eternal reward, and I had been left behind.

Another thing that frightened me was the dark. I hated to be shut in my bedroom after the lights were turned out because I was certain there were tigers out in the passage waiting to get me. I could hear them panting outside the bedroom door as I lay there holding my breath in fear. It was not until years later that I realised that it was my own heartbeat that I could hear.

For our summer holidays we caught a ship to Tsingtao (pronounced ching dow, as in how) by the seaside. We stayed at a rest home for Salvation Army officers and spent days on the beach or off in the country on donkey rides. We always had our servants with us to attend to the everyday necessities of life such as cooking and housekeeping and preparing our picnic lunches. Sometimes, if the mood possessed me I'd help the servants make peanut butter. Peanuts were very cheap, for a few cents you'd get a large sackful. We'd shell the nuts and remove the red skins, then put the nuts through a hand mincer. It took three or four goes to produce the smooth fine peanut paste which we spooned into screw-topped bottles. A sackful of peanuts would keep us in peanut butter for weeks.

There was a small pond outside the rest home where the frogs would serenade long into the summer nights. One of my parents' fellow officers, a German Captain Hugo Wessels—Uncle Wessels to us—found the frog song tedious, so one evening he poured kerosene over the pond and set it alight. Much to our intense amusement the frogs sang louder than ever as the flames licked skywards. I think we had a different sense of humour from that of my parents' German colleague.

Mum bought me an albino angora rabbit. He was a big fluffy cuddly ball and I kept him in a small hutch at the back of the holiday house. When it was time to return to Shanghai we had to devise a way of smuggling the rabbit past the shipping authorities, so we hit on the idea of carrying him in a wicker picnic basket. Mum carried the basket as we joined the line of passengers waiting to board the ship, resisting all offers from Chinese and Foreigners alike to carry it for her—it was unthinkable that a Foreign woman would carry anything! As we stood in line it became apparent that the wait had proved too long for the rabbit when an American gentleman said to Mum: 'Excuse me ma'am but your lemonade bottle's leaking'.

During our 1939 holidays in Tsingtao, World War II broke out and shortly afterwards my father was posted to Chungking, where Generalissimo Chiang Kai-shek had set up his administration. Chungking was a war zone so we would not be allowed to accompany Dad there. He left Shanghai on a grimy old Chinese tramp steamer bound for Hong Kong from whence he flew to Chungking in a twin engined Douglas airliner. Down at the Bund the Foreign and Chinese Salvation Army officers gave him a splendid sendoff. Their band played as we waved farewell and watched our coloured paper streamers part as the fussy little tugs worried the ship out into midstream, where it turned slowly and headed out to sea.

After my father left we moved to Tientsin where my mother took up the position as assistant matron at a hostel for the children of Salvation Army missionaries who were stationed in remote or dangerous places. There were about twenty five kids at the hostel and we all went to the Tientsin Grammar School which, like the Cathedral School, was affiliated with Cambridge University. Most of the teachers came from England and most of the students were British.

I was disappointed because I'd hoped that we might have been sent as boarders to Cheefoo. I don't remember what the attraction of Cheefoo was other than the fact that lots of our friends went there so I wanted to go there too. It was somewhere up north and they travelled back and forth by sea. On one trip back for the holidays, their ship had been boarded by pirates. The details of the attack are all pretty hazy in my mind but I rather fancied the drama of being ordered to hove to by a lumbering junk, with pirates swarming over the side, cutlasses clenched in their teeth. Do they really do that? I suppose I'll never know.

All the girls from the hostel joined the Brownies or Guides and the boys, the Cubs or Scouts, where we learned about knots and first-aid and cooking and tracking and went off on treks with trek carts and lit camp fires. Once we even went camping. Pulling trek carts, loaded with camping equipment and supplies, as we tramped the couple of miles out to the racecourse, where we pitched our tents before lighting a fire to cook our evening meal.

Half way through our meal the storm hit. The lightning flashed across the dark sky as the thunder crashed round us, and it started to rain, softly at first then in torrents. The racecourse was soon awash and our inexpertly pitched tents sagged and collapsed under the weight of water. Our leaders decided to abandon the camp so we collected our belongings and bolted for the grandstands where we huddled together for the rest of the night.

In the morning we packed up what remained of our belongings, loaded them onto our trek carts and trudged back to the Scout hall where we spread our things out to dry. I never got to go on another Cub camp.

CHAPTER 4

TIENTSIN HOSTEL

Set behind a high wall, the hostel was a three storey grey brick building with a two storeyed annex at the rear. It was a stately home that had been converted for our use, the seven-foot-high brick wall with its massive gates had broken glass cemented into the top to discourage break-ins. I slept in a dormitory on the top floor with six other boys of about my age. The older boys slept in the annex and the girls had a couple of rooms on the first floor. The dining room was on the ground floor. It had an enormous black baronial table which could seat more than thirty people. There was a whistling canary in a bamboo cage that hung from one of the windows. Folding doors opened into the sitting room where there was a large fireplace with a marble hearth, a piano and several generous brown leather armchairs. On blustery, wintry evenings we'd pull the chairs close to a roaring coal fire, or have a singsong around the piano accompanied by the older girls, some of whom were quite competent pianists.

At the hostel we were visited by the usual procession of hawkers, conjurers and magicians who spread their wares in the grounds to tempt us or performed for our entertainment. Tailors called to measure us for suits and bring them back a few days later ready to wear. If the fit wasn't quite what had been expected, which was often the case, any complaints were invariably met with an infuriating 'Char bu dor'—the Chinese equivalent of 'near enough' or 'she'll be right'.

When the shoemaker called he'd draw an outline of our feet on a sheet of brown paper then return a week or two later with shoes that fitted perfectly and never had to be broken in because he'd made allowance for every lump and bump, corn and bunion. Once a week Madame Sounrine, a white Russian refugee, came to give us piano lessons and told us we had 'piano fingers' then berated us for not doing enough practice and rapped our knuckles with a heavy black ruler. Periodically she'd have excruciating little concerts at her apartment where we had to render our latest achievements on a grand piano that was so large I had to sit on a cushion on the revolving piano stool with my legs dangling high above the pedals, trying desperately to keep the stool from spinning while I wrestled with the intricacies of 'Little Playmates'. When I got too lost, or if the piano stool elected to gyrate, I'd have to stop and restart in the middle. As the final note sounded, I'd slip to the floor and bolt for the solace of the corridor, to wait with the other budding impresarios for the presentation of our certificates and the afternoon tea.

Across the road from the hostel was Min Yuan, a large sports ground and playing field where we'd kick a football in winter or set up a wooden crate to serve as cricket stumps in summer. In the springtime when the equinoctial gales brought clouds of dust swirling across the city and filled the air with the litter of the streets, straw, leaves and myriad scraps of paper, we'd fly our kites. The Chinese were great kite fliers and for a few cents at the market you could buy the most exotic creations, dragonflies, butterflies, flying crickets and dragons.

But like all youngsters we wanted a pet of some sort. The canary was pretty impersonal. What we needed was a dog or a horse, or a flight of pigeons, or a monkey like the one our friend had tethered to a pole outside his bedroom window, where it climbed up and down from the yard to his window sill. After much cajoling the matron agreed to let us buy some tortoises. They were small, relatively easy to manage and shouldn't cause too much trouble.

We were delighted, although Mum hated the creatures. Their extended necks reminded her too much of snakes, and she'd had her fill of them in India where she'd once confronted a cobra in her dining room. But we boys thought the tortoises were good fun. We had tortoise races along the passage. On the wooden floor their shells would go klonk, klonk, klonk as they struggled laboriously along. Of course matron laid down strict rules. We had to feed and clean up after the tortoises, and they had to be in their boxes before bedtime.

47

At about two o'clock one morning Mum was wakened by the characteristic klonk, klonk, klonk of a tortoise on the wooden floor. Those wretched tortoises, she thought, and tried to go back to sleep, but the noise persisted.

She got out of bed, walked to the door, switched on the light and saw a man's foot protruding from under the bed. Thinking it was one of us after the tortoise she ordered,

'Come out from under that bed at once'.

To her horror a Chinese man appeared from under the bed pointing what appeared to be a gun at her. She turned and ran screaming from the room. Wisely, the burglar fled.

The police were called and by the time a British police officer, arrived there were about twenty five of us in our pyjamas draped down the banisters. He took one look at my mother, then at us and exclaimed in disbelief: 'Good God woman. All yours?'

The nearest holiday resort was at Pei Ta Ho Beach. Like Tsingtao there was a large rest home but this one was set in a spacious compound within easy walking distance of the beach. There were a couple of tennis courts and two or three summer houses in the park-like grounds where the servants served us cool drinks in the heat of the day.

Most of our time we'd spend swimming, fishing or playing tennis. On Sundays when it was not acceptable to play games, we'd go for long walks. In the evenings after dinner was served we'd sit on deckchairs out on the lawns, watching giant spiders weaving webs that were strong enough to catch small birds, between the cypress trees. Then, by the light of kerosene lamps we'd be sent off to bed. We loved our times at Pei Tai Ho but eventually we'd have to head off to the railway station for the trip back to Tientsin. The train services in North China were not noted for sticking to their timetables. At the station we'd jump down to the tracks and put our ears against the rails to hear if the train was coming. Eventually the train chuffed and puffed up to the platform. The locomotive had a shiny brass bell on top that tolled as the train crept hissing towards us through clouds of white steam.

We travelled second-class which was in the middle of the train and rather crowded, though we always had a seat. The rich people travelled first-class where there was much more room and the seats

With my mother, when I still had my golden curls.

The Salvation Army Territorial headquarters at 71 Morrison Street, Peking.
We lived in a compound at the rear of the building.

Under the grape vine at Ping Arn Farng, Peking, with my mother, sister and brother

An old Chinese man with his songbird

Chen Mun – the main gate through the Peking city wall. Some of the market
stalls can be seen on the left.

A favorite place of childhood: the Marble Boat at the Summer Palace, Peking.

Rickshaws at the entrance to the general market at Si Pilo.

Above and below: Refugees – victims of years of war.

Below: Some of the unwanted babies, always girls, at the babies' home in Shanghai

In our Cathedral School uniforms.
I am wearing the Girls' School crest on my blazer.

were a lot more comfortable. There were also a couple of deluxe suite-type compartments at the front of the train that were used mainly by very wealthy Chinese. There weren't too many Foreigners who were as well off as the really wealthy Chinese. At the back of the train were the third-class carriages. Chinese peasants crammed into these with their chickens, ducks, geese and sometimes even their goats and pigs. The carriages would be crowded beyond belief with people, animals and luggage packed in everywhere. People slept under seats and on the luggage carriers. Those who couldn't get into the carriages clung desperately from doors and windows, sat on the buffers between the carriages, or precariously on the roof where they were often wiped off as the train passed through tunnels.

On one trip back to Tientsin during an exploration through the first class section with my brother, we heard a commotion of some sort with a crowd gathered at one end of the carriage so we pushed through to see what was going on. At the end of the corridor a Japanese man dressed in a plain white kimono was kneeling on a white mat, a black sash around his shaved head with ties that hung down over his left ear. In front of him were, among other things, a small pottery bowl and an ornate looking dagger pointing towards him. The handle of the dagger was bound with a black silk cord. His eyes looked glazed and he seemed to be in some kind of trance. As he knelt with his hands resting on his thighs he spoke in a dull monotone.

We watched, not knowing quite what to expect. After a short while the talking stopped. He reached forward deliberately, grasped the dagger with both hands and held it pointing towards his lower abdomen. He paused for a moment. Then drawing the dagger towards him, he plunged it deep into his stomach, moved it around, up and across, then with a forward flick of his wrist disembowelled himself. For what seemed like an eternity he knelt there, glazed eyes staring into a nothingness in front of him, then slowly leaned forward and collapsed in the mess of blood and intestines on the mat.

Terrified, we pushed our way through the crowd and ran back to our compartments where we sat not daring to say a word. I'd not seen anyone commit harakiri before.

Back in Tientsin we'd get occasional letters from my father – mail deliveries in China were far from reliable. He told of the air raids in Chungking when they'd have to hide in underground shelters as the bombs exploded above them, and how they looked forward to cloudy nights when the city could not be seen from the air. He also told us about his work with the Generalissimo and Madame Chiang Kai-shek. With one letter came the news that he was to be moved to Hong Kong which, the authorities suspected, would soon be under threat of invasion by the Japanese as the war escalated. The British authorities had already evacuated most of the British women and children from the colony, so we would not be allowed in but would have to stay at the hostel.

Shortly after his arrival, my father learnt that auxiliary war nurses could get into Hong Kong, so my mother underwent training as nurse. A few months later we tearfully bade her farewell as she boarded a ship and we were left behind at Tientsin to continue our schooling.

It was a bit traumatic at first but we soon settled into the parentless world that all the other kids shared. It was so long since I'd seen my father I could barely remember what he was like, but I missed my mother a lot at first. However young memories are short and soon I was caught up with school and sports and piano practice and Cubs.

Queen Victoria's birthday, Empire Day, was celebrated on 24 May. It was a public holiday with school sports on Min Yuan—foot races, high and long jumps and all sorts of other athletic events. At the prize giving we got a speech, from an important-looking English official, about the might and greatness of the British Empire and medals to commemorate the occasion. As Australians we were part of the Empire. We were British and very proud of it. We'd often been told that the sun never set on the British Empire, and looking at all the parts on the atlas that were coloured red you could see that that was true. We sang patriotic songs confident in the knowledge that Britannia ruled the waves and deserved so to do. The war couldn't last long and it would only be a very short time before Hitler was brought to his knees. 'God is on our side. God is for the right and the right will win!'

I suppose I must have learnt something at school in Tientsin. I recall that I was introduced to the charm of *The House at Pooh Corner*, and also to *Black Beauty*. We were taught to weave on small looms and learnt a poem:

I saw the farmer plough the field
While row on row the furrows grow . . .

We had a White Russian girl in the class called Sonia. There were a large number of White Russians in North China who had fled across Siberia from the revolution. Many of them were destitute having been fortunate to escape with their lives and took whatever jobs they could find to keep themselves from starvation. Sonia had trouble with the pronunciation of plough, reciting the poem in a singsong fashion, 'I saw the farmer pluff the field . . .'

On Sundays we went to Sunday school where our superintendent, Eric Liddell, was our hero, He'd won the gold medal at the Olympic Games for the 400 metres (440 yards) and on the walls there were pictures of the race, and of him with a laurel wreath around his neck. We all knew the story of how he'd refused to race in the 100 yards because the heat was scheduled for Sunday: he'd even resisted the entreaties of the Prince of Wales to reconsider his stand. Instead he'd entered in the 440. A fellow competitor at the start of the race had given him a slip paper which said 'Them that honour me I will honour'. He'd run and he'd won. Years later they made a movie about him and called it *Chariots of Fire.*

As Foreigners we kept ourselves quite apart. We were surrounded and far outnumbered by Chinese but we had little to do with them and, apart from our servants, dealt with them only as tradesmen or shopkeepers. We took it for granted that coolie labour was used for everything, that all menial tasks were done by Chinese and that the average life expectancy of a rickshaw boy was twenty-eight years. What did it really matter that there were 450 000 000 of them and most of them were starving? Chinese did our housework, washed and ironed our clothes, prepared, cooked and served our meals. The only thing we were required to do for ourselves was clean and polish our shoes: this was, for some obscure reason, considered good for building character. We grew up in the unshakeable knowledge that mixed marriages were not to be condoned under any circumstance, that Eurasians were a lower form of life because they inherited the worst traits of both races and were looked down on by Chinese and Foreigners alike. As Foreigners we were superior and accepted the fact without question.

We learnt from the BBC news that things weren't going too well for the Allies in Europe. England was fighting for her life so we did everything we could to help the British War Fund. We attended fundraising functions which for some obscure reason were called Red Dog Nights and saved all our silver paper and bits of aluminium to send to England to make planes to replace those shot down defending 'That precious jewel tossed on a silver sea'. Hitler was the devil incarnate. All Germans were evil and must be stopped. Mussolini was a joke—his Eytie armies had demonstrated that they could run better than they could fight. The French had let us down when their Maginot Line collapsed, letting Paris fall into the hands of the Nazis.

It was up to British Empire to save the world. We sang 'We're going to hang out the washing on the Siegfried Line' with great gusto, but we had no idea what or where the Siegfried Line was.

CHAPTER 5

COMING OF THE JAPANESE

I ran down the uneven footpath, dodging wheelbarrows, handcarts and street stalls. Sidestepping hawkers wearing conical hats of woven bamboo, and carrying long poles across their shoulders from which hung huge bamboo baskets, filled with all manner of curious things for sale. Bundles of firewood, heaps of coal balls, vegetables, ironmongery, live chickens, ducks, pigs and even young children. I ran on past lorries that were being loaded or unloaded by files of coolies their backs bent under enormous loads, and chanting a monotonous, 'Aiya ho, oha ho. Aiya ho, oha ho' in rhythm with the unerring tread of the straw-rope sandals on their feet.

It was 8 December and although the sun was shining, the north wind was bitingly cold. It hadn't yet snowed—that would come later—but the pools of water on the footpath and in the muddy gutters had turned to ice. I had no way of knowing that this day would go down in history as one of the most infamous of the twentieth century. Across the date line on the other side of the world it was the morning of Sunday 7 December 1941. The unsuspecting, unprepared United States Pacific Fleet was anchored at the naval base of Pearl Harbor in the idyllic Hawaiian Islands. Out of the rising sun came the Japanese planes like birds of prey, swooping, diving, bombing, strafing. When their mission of destruction and havoc was done, the pride of the US fleet was immobilised. Palls of black smoke belched from stricken ships as they lay broken in the harbour many of them sinking or already sunk—they'd never had a chance. Hundreds of young men died with those ships, and many more were horribly wounded. Japan's unheralded, unprovoked and cowardly attack brought about America's entry into World War II. The Pacific War had started.

Oblivious of this, I ran on. My concern was that I might be late for school, and that usually spelt trouble.

Brigadier McKenzie was the matron of the hostel and a strict disciplinarian. We all called her 'Auntie Kenzie'. The missionaries were the only extended family we had and were known to us as 'uncle' or 'auntie' and followed by their surname, not their Christian name. Each morning before school we had to parade in front of Auntie in two rows for inspection, hands extended, palms down. She'd check our school uniforms, our shoes, our knuckles and fingernails for grime, then single one of us out to be sent back to wash our hands properly. The offender would go to the bathroom, wait for a couple of minutes, then return to be greeted with, 'That's much better, why couldn't you do that the first time?' In her fifties, she had angular features and a ruddy complexion, with small round silver-rimmed pince-nez glasses wobbling on the end of her sharp nose. Usually she dressed in a grey uniform and wore her snow-white hair pulled back in a bun. She claimed to be little hard of hearing but had an uncanny knack of being able to pick up anything that was whispered at the dinner table when talking was not allowed.

This Monday morning it was my turn to be sent back to the bathroom. If I was late for school, I faced the prospect of some sort of detention from the teachers, probably a hundred lines of 'I must not be late for school' or even 'Punctuality not tardiness', though I wasn't really sure what either word meant. Another favourite – 'Procrastination is the thief of time'—was a total mystery.

As I rounded the corner I could see the school building set behind its fence of tall steel pickets that looked like green spears with their arrow tips. The Tientsin Grammar School was a large, three-storeyed, grey brick structure with classrooms on both sides of wide corridors. Most of the yard was covered in asphalt with netball posts dotted here and there, climbing frames and monkey bars made of steel pipe, and a roundabout that stood like a maypole with ropes hanging from it. Through the six-foot-high steel pickets I was relieved to see that the other children were still milling in the yard. In fact the teachers seemed to be having trouble exercising control. Something was amiss, the place seemed confused. Then I noticed the large cast-iron schoolyard gates had been swung closed. Two soldiers in padded khaki Japanese uniforms with little cloth peaked caps on their heads stood guard outside the gates, weapons at the ready. They wore those funny black rubberised canvas ankle-length boots that Japanese soldiers wore which separated the big toe from the rest of the foot, and carried Mausers—large curious-looking pistols that could fold out to become rifles.

Hesitantly I walked towards the gate and tried to edge past the soldiers. A rifle butt swung up, catching me just above the right eye. Terrified, I turned and fled back to the hostel, my vision blurred by the mixture of tears and blood that streamed down my face and over my school blazer.

I was nine years old.

By now Jap soldiers were everywhere. Some marched down the middle of the road in a funny sort of half-walk, half-jog that was typical of them. Others, wielding bamboo sticks, moved along the footpaths lashing out at anyone within reach. Chinese screamed in terror, covering their heads with their arms to avoid the flaying clubs, as they fled before the mass of khaki uniforms.

Somehow I made it back to the hostel. A large paper seal had been pasted across the massive double oaken gates. I banged on the knocker, calling out to the gatekeeper to let me in. Through the security peephole he told me that he daren't break the seal, it had been put there by Japanese soldiers.

'Go back to school,' he shouted to me, 'Kwai kwai di poa! Run quickly!'

But the way back was blocked by the advancing Japanese troops surging down the road towards me, so I ducked around a corner and ran breathlessly on to Min Yuan. I had often played hide and seek here on Saturdays and I knew all the good hiding places. With my handkerchief and a piece torn from my shirt, I tried to staunch the bleeding from the gash above my eye—the way I'd been taught to do it in the cubs. As my breathing slowed and the sobs subsided I became aware of a dull headache from the blow of the rifle butt. Gingerly, I fingered the large lump that was forming on my forehead and wondered if it had started to turn blue.

I used to come here to fly kites with the other boys from the hostel, Of course our kites weren't like the fighting kites or the dragon kites that the Chinese men flew. The dragon kites were enormous, over thirty feet long and made of twenty or so discs of rice paper about two feet in diameter joined together at the edges to form a long cylinder. The first disc, which was larger than the others, had the face of a fearsome dragon painted on it. The other discs had a leg protruding from each side, usually covered in feathers, while a tail waved from the last section. It often took eight or ten men to get one of these kites into the sky and when it was up on a windy day it needed two or three men to control it. I loved the dragon kites and hoped one day to learn how to fly one.

Fighting kites were different. They were more like the ones we flew only bigger, the main difference being that several feet of the string nearest to the kite were coated with crushed glass. In a fight the idea was to try to get your kite's string to cut that of your opponent's. The fliers were very skilful, putting their kites through swoops and banks and dives. A kite fight looked very much like the dogfights we'd watched between the Chinese and Japanese planes that had taken place during the ten years of the Sino Japanese war.

While I was dreaming about kites I noted that the bleeding on my head had stopped but I realised how cold I was. I checked to see if the coast was clear. There were a few Jap soldiers out in the street, but the playing field was deserted so I moved from my hideout and, crawling between the seats, got to the end of the row furthest from the street. Staying low, I moved stealthily around to the back of the grandstand into a patch of sunshine. It was quite pleasant with the warmth reflecting from the grey brick wall, so I lay down on the asphalt and started to plan my next move.

It was quite clear that we were going to have to do something to stop the Japanese advance. I'd wait until the bigger boys got out of school, then with Donald, Gordon and James (they were really old, about twelve or thirteen) my brother and all the others, who knows some of the girls may even want to come along too—we could get our bikes and spring a surprise attack on the Nips. When they saw us coming brandishing our cap guns and water pistols, some of which looked very realistic, they'd be sure to either run for their lives or surrender. I could see it all happening, and we'd be heroes and perhaps even be given medals by the King.

Oh drat, I remembered, my bike's got a flat tire and I haven't fixed it.

Meanwhile at the school the teachers had rounded up the students and marched them into the assembly hall where the Headmaster, wearing his mortarboard and gown, had addressed them from the stage, urging them to be calm and not show any sign of panic. 'You are British and must deport yourselves with pride and dignity,' he said. 'God is on our side, God is for the right, and the right will win. God Save the King!' He then led them in the singing of the school song, 'Gaudiamus igatur, juvenes dum sumus'.

After that a Japanese officer with a sword almost as big as himself—they were such little runts, these Nips—had mounted the podium and burst forth into a long tirade in Nipponese, which nobody understood. After the lecture, the head dismissed the assembly and told the students to go to their classes. There were Japanese soldiers in the corridors, and a couple of the younger lady teachers had been seized and dragged off. They returned sometime later, red eyed, their hair and clothing dishevelled, and although quite obviously shaken they maintained a strong and purposeful dignity. in front of their classes. Apparently there was a lot of laughter and buffoonery amongst some of the soldiers, who seemed to be enjoying themselves immensely.

An attempt was made to commence lessons, but these were frequently interrupted as soldiers barged into the classrooms, souveniring anything they fancied. Shortly afterwards a Japanese officer, attended by several others soldiers, entered each classroom and made an important-sounding proclamation in Japanese. Somehow the word was passed around that everyone was required to assemble in the schoolyard where another seemingly endless speech was given in Japanese by yet another high-ranking officer. Eventually the children were dismissed and told to return to their homes.

When the kids got back to the hostel there was a Jap guard at the gate who let them in, then closed and sealed the gate behind them.

Hidden away from the wind, I was now pleasantly warm but it was tiffin time—we called our midday meal tiffin—I was getting hungry and something would have to be done about that. Min Yuan was still deserted so, keeping as close as I could to the wall, I edged my way toward the main entrance. Finding that the street was also deserted, I made a dash for the small lane or hootung which was about half a block away and wound around to the back of the hostel. We boys had often climbed the three storeys up the heavy cast-iron rain-water down-pipe to the hostel roof. Auntie Kenzie used to get into a rage if she caught us, but I considered this to be an emergency and worthy of the risk. I scrambled up like a monkey, grazing my shins a couple of times. Once my school blazer caught on an iron bracket and gave an ominous ripping sound, but I made it to the roof. Gingerly I crept around until I found a spot where I knew I could lower myself down onto a verandah that surrounded an internal courtyard. From there it would be easy enough.

Finally I made it. I tiptoed down the back stairs to the kitchen, hoping that the cook would give me something to eat. He was usually pretty good that way, giving us titbits that Auntie Kenzie vowed would spoil our meals. But this time I was out of luck. When the cook saw me he let out a yell and my attempts to keep him quiet were to no avail. He grabbed me and rushed me up to Auntie Kenzie's office. I knew I was for it. I was filthy, my school uniform was torn and covered with blood so I'd wanted a chance to clean up before anyone saw me, but it was too late. To my amazement, instead of the usual lecture the poor old soul took me into her arms, cuddled and kissed me and dropped to her knees, where she offered up a prayer of thanks to God for my safe return. I wondered what I'd done to deserve this uncharacteristic display of attention. One of the amahs was summoned and I was sent off in her care to be cleaned up and have my head bandaged.

Usually everything about the hostel was ordered and disciplined but on this day order had deserted the place. The younger children were running up and down the stairs shouting to each other. Some of the boys were sliding down the banisters and no one seemed to mind. The telephones rang every few minutes but when you picked up the receivers all you heard was 'Mushee mushee, mushee mushee'. It was impossible to make outgoing calls.

The senior girls had all been confined to their rooms and were told that under no circumstance were they to be seen looking out the windows. Words I had never heard before like 'rape', 'molestation' and 'violation' were being whispered. From time to time arrogant strutting Japanese military officers would barge through the front doors unannounced. Swords swinging and clanking from their waists, their hobnailed boots gouged into the highly polished wood of the stately oak staircase. They'd be followed by retinues of varying sizes all shouting orders and pushing or cuffing anyone who was in their path.

One officer was particularly belligerent and when Auntie Kenzie tried to stop him from entering one of the rooms he felled her with a vicious blow. We watched terrified as his retinue stood guard at the door. When the officer emerged he aimed a kick at the inert body of Auntie Kenzie, then marched down the stairs and out of the hostel. Some of the Chinese servants rushed to Auntie's assistance while others ran in to comfort some of the girls who had become hysterical. We younger kids huddled on the landing above peering nervously through the balustrade not knowing what was expected of us or what we should do next.

The war wasn't going quite as I'd expected it should.

CHAPTER 6

SMALL BOY LOST

Life at the hostel returned to some sort of normalcy as visits from Japanese officers became less frequent. The telephones no longer worked but at least they'd stopped their incessant ringing. We were prisoners and not allowed outside the grounds but the Chinese staff were permitted to move freely, so they shopped for our provisions and brought us news of the outside world.

Towards the end of the week a high-ranking Japanese officer presented himself at the front door, knocked and courteously asked if he could speak to whoever was in charge. Auntie Kenzie, who had recovered from the blow she'd received a few days earlier, came to meet him and demanded in her broad Scottish accent what it was he thought he was about. The Japanese officer, speaking faultless English, advised that all children were to report to the school at nine o'clock on Monday morning to resume their studies. Just like that— as if nothing had happened. We kids didn't think that was much of an idea. While there was a war going on we thought that we had an excellent excuse for not going to school ever again and, besides, spending all day at school could seriously disrupt our plans for the overthrow of the Nipponese forces as soon as the opportunity presented itself. But officialdom prevailed and on Monday morning, despite our protests, off we went to school.

Tientsin was overrun with soldiers. Everywhere you looked, white flags with a red blob in the centre were flying from bamboo flagpoles. The Japanese called their flag the rising sun, but we thought it looked more like a poached egg and that's what we called it. Otherwise everything else was normal. Coolies still staggered under their backbreaking loads. Streetside food stalls, were, as ever, engulfed in clouds of white mist as rice steamed, or chowsers—which were

60

much like bowsers only cooked in a thin, clear soup—boiled fragrantly. Vendors, with enormous baskets suspended from bamboo poles carried across their shoulders, called out their wares but, worst of all for us, the school gates were open and in we went, as we had done on every other Monday morning of the school year. Who knows, the whole course of the war might have been changed if only we'd had the chance to stage our counter attack. By sending us back to school, the might of the Imperial Japanese Empire may have saved itself from certain defeat at our hands. History's great moments hang on such minutiae!

At nine o'clock we assembled in the grounds outside the main entrance, but now there was a poached egg at the masthead where the Union Jack had always flown. To the accompaniment of the 'Coronation March' from the Prophet, the teachers marched us straight up the stairs and into the assembly hall where the school choir was formed up on the stage. We took our places and sat in silence, nervously waiting, not knowing quite what to expect. Then in came the Head. With his mortarboard and flowing black gown, he looked even taller than his six foot four inches. We rose to our feet and stood to attention as we always did when he entered a room. He nodded briefly to the pianist and then, raising his right hand he began to sing:

> I give you a toast Ladies and Gentlemen,
> I give you a toast Ladies and Gentlemen,
> 'May this fair land we love so well
> In dignity and freedom dwell.'
> Tho worlds may change and go awry
> While there is still one voice to cry.

Then the choir joined in, softly at first, almost in a whisper, but their notes swelled in a gradual crescendo until we were swept up by the power of the song and added our voices to the singing:

> There'll always be an England
> Where there's a country lane,
> Wherever there's a cottage small
> Beside a field of grain.
> There'll always be an England

Where there's a busy street:
Wherever there's a turning wheel
A million marching feet.

Red white and blue,
What does it mean to you?
Surely you're proud,
Shout it aloud, Britons awake,
The Empire too, we can depend on you,
Freedom remains, these are the chains, nothing can break!

There'll always be an England
And England shall be free,
If England means as much to you
As England means to me.

When we resumed our seats the Head delivered a rousing message and finished by reiterating: 'Never forget, you are British and proud of it. God is on our side. God is for the right, and the right will win! God save the King!'

As we filed back to our classrooms the piano played 'The War March of the Priests'.

Our teachers immediately set us to work on patriotic projects and soon the school's walls were festooned with posters proclaiming the power and majesty of the British Empire. One I particularly remember was at the top of the stairs; it had an open nut cracker encircling a walnut that contained a map of the British Isles. The caption read 'A nut too hard to crack'.

We were exhorted to work even harder for the British War Fund. All old aluminium pots and pans were to be collected; all the silver paper we could get was carefully smoothed out then rolled into balls. This would be sent to England to build more planes for the war effort. The girls knitted socks for the soldiers at the front and the boys learnt to weave scarves. A euphoria gripped us all. It was obvious that the war couldn't possibly last more than a week or two—a couple of months at most. What possible chance could Japan have when confronted with the might of the British Empire?

It was speech day and the senior students, who had been rehearsing for a performance of the Mikado, decked themselves out in their kimonos for the dress rehearsal. The Japs thought that the performance was being staged in their honour. It was a heady week, but on Friday afternoon the school was again visited by a contingent of Japanese troops. They ripped the posters from the walls. They shouted, they kicked and they cuffed. We were ordered to collect our belongings and return to our homes. The school was to be turned into a military barracks.

The following week the Japs commandeered the hostel. It, too, was needed for a barracks, so we were all sent home. Well most of us were, but my sister, brother and I didn't have a home to go to. Our parents were still in Hong Kong and all communication and transport between North and South China had been cut. We were told that we'd be cared for by some missionary folk in Peking, so with our few belongings packed into a small suitcase we joined the largest contingent of children as they were herded down to the railway station to be loaded onto a freight train that was headed North.

Although there'd been a heavy frost in the night, the sun was now shining and it was pleasantly warm as it streamed through the bars of the freight truck. That was until the train started moving, and the icy wind bit into us, freezing our ears, fingertips and faces. Blue and crying from the aching pain of the bitter cold, we had no food and nothing to drink. We huddled closely together, shivering as chilblains formed on our fingers, toes and ears.

It was a slow trip. The train stopped and started and stopped, it shunted back, it shunted forward. Finally around four in the afternoon with much clanking and jolting it ground to a halt outside a small village. Our trucks were shunted onto a siding and the train went on without us. It was getting dark. We were frightened, frozen and terribly hungry. We'd had nothing to eat or drink since breakfast and the freight truck was becoming putrid from lack of toilet facilities.

Some time after dark a group of Chinese villagers came and brought us some boiled rice. It was warm and there was plenty of it, which raised our spirits. Then they passed in cups of hot Chinese tea. After we'd eaten they left us to whatever the night had in store.

Cuddling each other for warmth, we slept fitfully until just before dawn when we heard a train whistle in the distance. There was a heavy jolt as our carriage was hooked onto another train which slowly puffed on towards Peking. It was late afternoon before we reached the station. Japanese soldiers unlocked the freight truck, herded us into rows, then marched us along the platform to the main exit, where they ordered us to halt. A few minutes later they went away and left us. I'd wet my pants in the night and was almost wetting myself again so I ran off to find a toilet.

When I got back the others had gone. I found myself alone on the station, cold, frightened and very hungry.

Not quite sure what I should do next, I went back to the men's toilet to clean myself as best I could, then walked along the platform where, as inconspicuously as possible, I slipped into the waiting room which was crowded with Chinese who were squatting on their haunches around a cast-iron stove. It was noisy and the room reeked of a mixture of unwashed bodies and garlic, but it was warm so I found myself a spot behind the door where I hoped I would not be noticed if any soldiers came in and sat snuggled in the corner on the floor.

I was just dozing off when an elderly Chinese lady came over to me and asked in Mandarin what I was doing there. It must have been obvious that I was hungry, I suppose little boys are always hungry, for she offered me some mahn-to, a warm cornmeal cake, which I devoured. When I'd told her of my plight and said I had nowhere to go, she said that her train had been delayed for some hours so, after checking to see that the platform was clear of soldiers, she took me by the hand and led me out into the night. Her name was Chow Tai Tai and she'd once been amah to a young lad about my age. She led me down numerous streets and hootungs to her house, where she gave me into the charge of her family before bustling back to the station. I remember arriving there, sitting at the table to a hot meal, trying desperately to be polite so that neither I, nor they would lose face, but finding it impossible to stay awake.

Next morning I woke to find myself in a small room with a low ceiling that was papered with white rice paper. I was lying on a palliasse on the floor, which was covered with woven straw matting. There was intricately fretted wood work around the windows which were unglazed but coated with a coarse cheese cloth, white rice paper blinds were rolled across the windows. The doorway was also edged with darkly lacquered fret work. The house reminded me of Ping An Farng but it was much smaller and in a worse state of repair. There were several other palliasses on the floor each with a small cylindrical-shaped pillow, some neatly folded bedding and a pair of cloth sandals at their foot. Along one wall there was a traditional style Chinese bed. About table high it was built from bricks with a small opening at the front about one foot square. This was where a small fire could be lit in cold weather to heat the bricks and warm the bed. The room didn't have a door so I could see out into the kitchen, where the Kitchen God glowered down from his position behind the door. The Chow family were up and about. The men had gone off to work and the women were busy with cooking and cleaning. They made a great fuss over me when I came into the room and gave me some rice porridge for my breakfast, another piece of mahn-to and a cup of hot green tea. There was a small fire of coal balls burning in an open hearth. Seated on a three-legged stool, I huddled in front of this while I ate.

I had absolutely no idea what was to become of me and I didn't really care too much as long as I wasn't cold and I had something to eat. I wondered how long I would live here and whether I would become a Chinese. I'd probably have to wear Chinese clothes and maybe have my head shaved, as did most of the Chinese children I knew. I supposed the other kids from school would call me a Chink. This didn't worry me too much as my brother used to tell me that I was not actually a member of the family, but was in fact a White Russian refugee whom the family had rescued from the snow one winter's night. He said that my real name was Boris Apleeza-blankaploboff. The story had spread around the school and the hostel, so many of the kids called me Boris. I'd been taunted with it so often that I half believed it. After all, everyone said my sister looked like my father and my brother took after my mother. That left me the runt of the litter.

When I tried to speak to the ladies they laughed and hid their faces behind their hands. I knew they weren't laughing at my accent—my amah had taught me to speak Mandarin before I could speak English—so I guessed that they must have been embarrassed. I learnt that there were five Chow children, three boys and two girls. It was customary for the Chinese to give little girls charming names like

Lotus Flower or Fragrant Rose because no one wanted girls and they were thus safe from predation by the evil spirits. Not so little boys. Boys were in great demand so they were given imaginative names like Evil Smelling Dog or Repulsive Pig. With names such as these, they might be safe, for it was hoped that no self-respecting spirit, even an evil one, would want anyone with such a name. The boys of a family were seldom called by their names, instead they were numbered Di Yi, Di Urr, Di San (literally Number One, Number Two, Number Three) and so on down the line.

Di Urr was about my size and, though he claimed to be a couple of years older, was probably about the same age because Chinese children were considered to be one year old at birth and then attained another year at Chinese New Year when, like racehorses, all Chinese had a common birthday. Di Urr and I got on famously. He was anxious to try out the little English that he'd picked up around the streets. Most beggar children called out, 'No Mamma, no Papa, no whisky-soda', so he knew that one and also the little rhyme:

Me no savee, me no care
Me go marry a millionaire
If he die,
Me no cry,
Me go marry 'nurrer guy.

But he got his greatest enjoyment from slapping me on the shoulder and shouting, 'You are my sonofabitch'.

We played marbles, tops and hopscotch and made a shuttlecock so that we could have competitions to see how many times we could kick it before it fell to the ground. I was no match for him, although I could hold my own at marbles and hopscotch, and was able to give him a bit of a run around with ball games. I thought I was going to rather enjoy being a Chinese. There seemed to be plenty of food and no talk of unpleasant things like school or the war, though I did find the floor a bit uncomfortable to sleep on.

It had probably only been a day or so, but it seemed that I'd been there for weeks when a man arrived at the front door of the house. He said that he was Swiss, and that he represented the Red Cross. He told me that the Chows had made him aware of my predicament and that he been able to locate the missionary family who were looking after my brother and sister. He had no news of my parents, but told me that the fighting at Hong Kong had been very fierce and there had been a lot of casualties. Tearfully I took leave of the Chow family, told Di Urr that he was my sonofabitch, and set off in a rickshaw with the Red Cross man, for the other side of Peking. It was the day before Christmas Eve and it had started to snow.

CHAPTER 7

ORPHAN OF WAR

The Stensons had no doubt been beside themselves with worry but I don't think I sensed their concern. They were old friends of the family who had gone out to China in 1921 on the same ship as my parents. I'd met them several times, either when my parents had been stationed close to them, or at the summer rest houses where we stayed at Pei Ta Ho Beach or Tsingtao. Uncle Stenson was now the principal of a theological college in Morrison Street and as the place was closed for the Christmas break, my brother and I had beds in one of the large dormitories while my sister slept in the house with the family.

That night it was still snowing as we had dinner in a room cheerfully decorated for Christmas. A fir tree decked with tinsel and baubles stood in the corner of the sitting room with a heap of colourfully wrapped presents at its base.

After dinner we went Christmas carolling around the compound, singing outside the houses of the staff members. There was a lot of excitement as we gathered at doorways, our voices and mirth muffled by the soft falling snow. After we'd rendered the familiar carols we'd be invited in for cups of piping hot cocoa and sweets and cake, then amid calls of Merry Christmas we'd move on to the next house. By the time we got back to the Stensons' place we were exhausted and gorged with much eating and drinking. We couldn't imagine that it would be a long, long time before we'd again be sated with overindulgence.

Pulling off our mittens and shaking the snow from our coats and scarves, we went in to the glowing warmth of the hall. It was a family tradition that on Christmas Eve Uncle Stenson read aloud from Charles Dickens' A Christmas Carol, so we gathered in the sitting room around a glowing coal fire. All the lights were turned out except for one candle, and by its guttering light he began to read in measured tones: 'Marley was dead . . .'

Somewhere in the house a door slammed, a sudden gust of wind blew out the candle, weird shadows flitted across the walls chased by firelight.

With all that talk about ghosts I was terrified going back to the loneliness of the large dormitory. I lay in bed too frightened to breathe, yearning for the close comfort of Di Urr who'd slept beside me on the floor at the Chow's place. I could hear the measured breathing of the tigers out in the passage, and the stiller I lay the more certain I was that they were waiting to get me. They'd go away when my brother rolled over in his bed, but as soon as the room was quiet they were back again. At last I slept and when I woke it was Christmas morning.

It had stopped snowing and I could hear church bells ringing somewhere in the distance. Icicles hung from the gutters and Jack Frost had made ice patterns across the windowpanes. The outside world was covered in a mantle of white. My brother's bed was empty so I dressed and hurried down the passage to the large bathroom where I washed in the cold water I drew with a dipper from the large karng in the corner of the room. I combed my hair and ran across the yard to the house, hoping for some breakfast. The family was already gathered around the Christmas tree and Uncle Stenson, playing Father Christmas, was handing out presents. I was surprised to find there were some for me from the Stensons and other missionary families in Peking, but most amazingly there were presents from our parents, three of them for me: a Dick cap gun complete with caps, a chocolate-scented dog ball that bounced in a most incredible fashion and a tin of Mackintosh's Toffee. It appears that our parents had sent these presents some months earlier not knowing quite where they or we would be at Christmas time.

There was lots of talk about the war, but little was said about Hong Kong. I gathered that the news was not good because I had already gleaned that, although Kowloon had capitulated at the start of the war, Hong Kong itself had withstood the Japanese assault. The Japs had given an ultimatum that if the island had not surrendered by Christmas Day they would bring up their heavy artillery and 'blow it out of the sea'. It was not until months later that we heard that Hong Kong had fallen.

After opening our presents we all set off to the Union Church, where we sang carols and heard the Christmas story retold. It was an exciting day.

I soon settled into my life at the college and came to enjoy the freedom of the dormitory. We ate our meals with the Stensons unless they had visitors for dinner in which case my brother and I would eat in the kitchen with the servants. I spent more and more time with the servants and enjoyed helping the cook with the peanut butter. I found an old bicycle in a storage shed which the gatekeeper helped me fix, and I set off exploring Peking. Across the road from the training college was an opium den where old men would sit trance-like in the smoky gloom. Sometimes I'd peep through the curtains to watch them puffing away on long-stemmed pipes. I never saw a drunk Chinese. Alcoholic drinks didn't seem to be part of their culture. In Shanghai you could get EWO beer, and United Breweries UB beer but these seemed to be for consumption by Foreigners. The Chinese were into opium.

Although there was still no word about my parents, they had become so remote I seldom thought about them. I was too young for my brother to be bothered with. He had again told his friends that I was an adopted White Russian waif so they teased me about my background and called me Boris. However I had made a few friends of Foreign boys of my own age and as winter slowly gave way to spring and the warm sun softened the frozen earth and freed the daffodils and snowdrops, we spent more and more time out of doors.

We were having a great time, and as long as we avoided the Japanese soldiers we could go almost anywhere we wished, wandering all over Peking unchecked. Of course there was always the risk of being noticed by a Nip for some perceived or imagined misdemeanour. This resulted in a severe cuff about the ears followed by an hour or so of standing to attention in the street. The soldier would draw a chalk line around your feet then go about his duties. If he or one of his number saw that your foot had moved ever so slightly outside the chalk line you incurred more cuffing and another hour at attention. This treatment didn't cause too much trauma for we youngsters unless we were bursting to go to the toilet, which could prove embarrassing and often messy, but it was very trying for the older folk, especially in the very cold or very hot weather.

Mostly I kept out of trouble. Occasionally I'd drop around to see Di Urr or sometimes I'd wheel my bike up onto the city wall, where I could ride around looking down on the city. Sometimes, with my friends, I'd explore the markets at Dung Si Pilo and Chen Mun where, even if we didn't have the few coppers it took to buy what we wanted, we could watch the fortune-tellers and streetside magicians and apothecaries and pickpockets and beggars all plying their trade. In spite of the abominable smells, the food markets of Pig Street had a magnetic attraction. We loved to wander, looking at the tubs of live fish, the pigeons and other birds, the pigs, goats and rabbits, the huge containers filled with a limitless assortment of goldfish, the chickens, the ducks and the large pink geese. Pink geese brought good luck, so for a few weeks before wedding time a goose with feathers dyed pink would wander around the yard of the bride-to-be. Weddings in China were arranged by the parents and the young couple frequently met for the first time on their wedding day. In spite of this, or perhaps because of it, the system worked.

Often we'd cycle over to Pei Hai or the Summer Palace with its Marble Boat and the humpbacked and zigzag bridges, or to the Temple of Heaven where the reflection from the dragon carved in the ceiling had burnt itself into the marble floor directly below it. Or to the nearby Altar of Heaven which Chinese believed was the centre of the world. China to the Chinese is Djung Gao—literally central nation. Peking was the central city of China and the altar, which was built in circular fashion from large marble blocks, was the centre of Peking, in other words the centre of the world. The curious thing about it was that if you stood on the centre marble block—the very centre of the Earth—your voice echoed; if you stood anywhere else on the altar it didn't.

One of my friends was Alfred Wessels, son of the very Nazi Captain Hugo Wessels. Alfred was about my age and an active member of the Hitler Youth. Dressing up in his brown uniform with a swastika on the sleeve he'd throw Fascists salutes accompanied by a shouted 'Heil Hitler'. Uncle Wessels had a short-wave radio with a 'magic eye' in the middle of the dial—it was a round green light like an iris that opened and closed to indicate if you were tuned into the station. Several times a day he'd excuse himself and go off to his room to listen to the news from Germany. Sometimes Alfred and I would listen too. Uncle Wessels would sit with his ear pressed against the set anxious lest he should miss a word of the broadcast but muttering under his breath the while, 'Come on Adolf, get zem, get zem. Ziek Heil. God iss on our side, ve vill vin.'

One day when I was at their house Uncle Wessels opened his desk drawer to find a nest of mice had taken up residence there. I was appalled to see him catch the little furry balls in his bare hands, and crush the life out of them.

During the cold winter months we'd not seen much of the Japs, but like insects they seemed to be attracted out by the sun and warmth. A contingent arrived at the college one morning to announce that it would not be allowed to reopen, that henceforth the city was to be placed under martial law and a curfew would be imposed. Anyone found on the streets after 6 p.m. without a special permit would be shot.

We enemy nationals were issued with identification cards, which were to be carried at all times, and coloured armbands which we had to wear if we were away from our own homes. We were obliged to bow whenever we saw a Japanese soldier, and to remain standing with head bowed until he'd passed. It was frequently impressed upon us that Japan's glorious Emperor had taken a special interest in our well-being and that we should be grateful to the him for his concern.

None of this was too onerous. The ID cards were no hardship, and as for the armbands which were intended to make us lose face in the eyes of the Chinese, they proved to be a bonus. When we entered a shop wearing the red armbands that signified we were British, the Chinese treated us with far more consideration than they did other nationals. Food was very scarce in the shops, but extra titbits or delicacies that our American, Scandinavian, French or Spanish friends believed to be unobtainable, would appear from under the counter.

Uncle Stenson was concerned that our education was being neglected and he prevailed upon the Mother Superior of a Roman

Catholic Convent, Mother Margaret-Kathleen, to allow my sister, his daughter and some other girls to attend there as day students. Mother Margaret-Kathleen willingly agreed, aware that she would have incurred severe punishment if the Japanese authorities learnt that she had enemy nationals on the premises. Most of the nuns were very helpful, and two in particular took a special interest in these girls. There were, however, those who strongly resented the girls' presence and did all they could to make life miserable for them. One of the nuns was a German and two were Irish. Frequently the Japanese would spring surprise raids on the college, but somehow Mother Margaret-Kathleen's intelligence system warned her and she'd spirit the girls out the back door just before the Nips burst in. The soldiers would be furious and on one occasion gave several nuns a severe beating.

Next day Mother Margaret-Kathleen called on Uncle Stenson. Her face was swollen and an eye was blackened. In spite of Uncle Stenson's protests Mother Margaret-Kathleen insisted that the girls return to the convent.

'Sure an' we'll not let them beat us,' she said grinning at him through cracked lips. Then giving us a broad wink she went on in her wide brogue 'And Oi'll be tellin' ya this, and sure it's the truth, ya cannot trust them Oirish!'

Another family friend, Captain Nel Bristow—actually I think I was named after her—assumed responsibility for my education. She'd had no teaching background but, armed with a copy of Arthur Mee's Children's Encyclopaedia, she captivated my interest with lessons on natural history. From its pages she taught me many of the wonders of nature and introduced me to the fascinating world of insects, snakes, birds and spiders.

There was an American missionary compound in Peking and the residents there, with sons who called their mothers 'Marmy' and their fathers 'Sir', set up a small school along American lines so I was transferred from the loving care of Auntie Bristow to the curious ways of the American school. I learnt to spell 'color' and 'flavor' without a 'u'. No doubt there were other academic pursuits, but all that I remember was learning to play basketball and softball, what crabapples were and how to make crabapple jelly. I think the crabapple skills were wasted on me.

Then one day a telegram arrived from my parents. Concerned about the progress of the war in Europe and the way things were shaping up in China, they had decided that we children should be sent home to Australia for the duration of the war in Europe. The telegram was dated November 1941, it had taken five months to reach us!

Passages had been booked for us on a ship that was to sail from North China on 6 December and would take us to Hong Kong, whence we would proceed to Sydney. The ship we were to have caught was sunk with no survivors.

A couple of months later we had another visit from the Red Cross to tell us that our parents had been located. They were being held in the Stanley Internment Camp on Hong Kong Island. A Red Cross representative had visited them, informing them of our whereabouts and that we were all well. Our parents until then had supposed us to have perished when they'd heard that our ship had been sunk. For eight months they'd assumed that we were dead.

In an attempt to reunite our family the Red Cross had drawn-out negotiation with the Japanese that went on for months and months. Meanwhile things in Peking became less pleasant. There'd been a severe drought throughout the region and food was pretty scarce. Fields and gardens were parched as hot winds blew in blinding red dust storms from the Gobi Desert that engulfed the city. The missionaries called for a day of prayers for rain to be followed by a prayer meeting in the Salvation Army's main meeting hall at seven o'clock that night. At the appointed hour the Chinese started to arrive, most of them with umbrellas and some even carrying galoshes.

What did they expect, rain? None of the missionaries was naive enough to have brought an umbrella.

The meeting commenced. A couple of the missionaries offered prayers for rain, then some of the Chinese started to raise their voices in prayer. There was a flash of lightning. A clap of thunder, then another. Soon the rain started to fall. It drummed on the roof and streamed down the windows. The meeting had to be disbanded because of the din of the storm and some of the missionaries got very wet going home that night.

When the rains came and the young crops were starting to sprout, a locust plague stripped the fields and North China faced the prospect of famine. Peking swarmed with locusts. We caught them in their thousands and our cook prepared them for us in various ways— roasted on top of the stove, or fried in deep fat with spring onions— and we learned to enjoy them. They tasted rather nutty and it beat being hungry.

Peking is very hot in summer and during those long languid days my wanderings often took me to visit the British Legation for a dip in their swimming pool. The legation wall had been stormed and breached during the Boxer Rebellion at the beginning of the century and although a new wall had been built inside the old one, the crumbling old wall still stood with 'Lest We Forget' painted on it in large black letters.

Eventually the Red Cross persuaded the Japanese authorities to have our parents released from Stanley Camp on Christmas Eve 1942, and sent by ship to Shanghai. Early in 1943, we children were granted permission to travel by train from Peking to Shanghai accompanied by Major Dorthe, a Salvation Army Officer who, as a Swiss national, was a citizen of a neutral country. I believe that we were the last enemy nationals to travel on the Chinese rail system until the end of the war.

It was a long, slow, uncomfortable journey as the trains were falling into serious disrepair. Back then the Japanese were not noted for their skill as engineers or mechanics. They believed that the machines were driven by some sort of benevolent spirit, or perhaps a malevolent one, so the engines constantly broke down and we'd sit for hours in the middle of nowhere waiting for a replacement. It was winter again and freezing cold. Frequently the train wheels found it difficult to find a grip and the slow chuff, chuff, chuff of the engine would rise to a wild chatter as the driving wheels skidded on the icy tracks. As always the train was crowded with people, chickens, ducks, geese, pigs, goats and bundles of belongings that were crammed into corridors and hanging from luggage racks. Extra passengers sat on the roofs of carriages or perched precariously outside the train hanging onto doors and windows.

At every station, we were searched. The procedure was always the same, we'd be ordered to clamber over the clutter and present ourselves on the platform, where we would bow to the soldiers and wait with heads bowed as Uncle Dorthe offered our papers for inspection. The soldiers would examine them with a great show of care, although usually holding them upside down or sideways, then burst forth into a long dissertation in Japanese none of which I understood. Uncle Dorthe who had some knowledge of the language, waited until the lecture lost some of its momentum, and would then interrupt to explain that he was Swiss and we children were Australian. Austrian? Ah so! The Japs would suck air noisily through their teeth several times, nodding their comprehension and approval. That was different. We were not enemy at all but on their side, suck, suck, hiss, hiss. We did little to disabuse them; all's fair in love and war. I wasn't much of an authority on love but I was starting to learn about war.

Early the next morning we were again ordered off the train. This time because we had come to a river crossing and the bridge had been blown up. We had to clamber down the muddy embankment and into small boats that ferried us across to the other side where another train was waiting. But instead of letting us board the train, soldiers took the four of us to a large tin shed where we were again interrogated thoroughly. We had with us a portable typewriter and this seemed to cause the interrogating soldiers considerable concern. The questioning went on and on, the typewriter was examined, poked and prodded. It was tipped on its side, it was tipped upside down. To our dismay we heard the whistle blow and the train move on without us. We spent all day in that dirty, freezing hut with little food or water, undergoing hours of questioning.

Late in the afternoon a Japanese officer came into the shed, picked up the typewriter, said something to the soldiers, then nodding his head and grinning at us he said, 'Nippon have, Nippon have.' At that he tucked the typewriter under his arm and marched out the door. We never saw him or the typewriter again.

Shortly afterwards another train arrived. The Jap soldiers forced a space for us in one of the carriages and we were on our way again.

Finally we made it to Shanghai. It was evening when the train pulled into the station. There we underwent more interrogations and tirades, but at last we were allowed to go. A Chinese who obviously did not want to be caught talking to Foreigners in a public place, sidled up to Uncle Dorthe, said 'Follow me', and walked out to a waiting rickshaw. We hailed one of the many rickshaws that swarmed around the station gate, and after bargaining and agreeing on a price, set off in pursuit of the mysterious stranger. As usual the streets of Shanghai were crammed with rickshaws, cars, buses, tramcars, trolley-busses, handcarts, wheelbarrows, myriads of bicycles, dogs and people while the footpaths were lined with beggars, and the air was filled with the customary shouting, blaring of horns and clanging of bells.

Our Chinese guide, who it transpired, was himself a Salvation Army officer and had been awaiting our arrival at the station for three days, led us to Yang Terrace where we arrived as night was falling. My parents were waiting at the door—somehow word had got to them that we had at last arrived—and it was a strange reunion, I hadn't seen my mother for two years and it was close to four since I'd seen my father. I wasn't really sure that I'd know who they were.

As my mother gathered me in her arms my first question was: 'Mummy, am I Boris Apleezablankaploboff?'

CHAPTER 8

PRISONERS AGAIN

'Of course you're not,' Mum said as she took me in here arms and gave me a big cuddle. 'What on earth gave you that silly idea?'

Apart from the time that Auntie Kenzie had hugged me after my return to the hostel, this was the first time anyone had embraced me for two years. Mum was warm and comforting and I liked the smell of her. I'd forgotten how nice a cuddle could feel.

'My haven't you grown,' father said. I wondered what he had expected. After all I was only seven when he'd seen me last and now I was ten.

We were ushered up the stairs into a large sitting room with high ceilings and a rather worn rug on the timber floor. Thick velvet curtains covered the windows and a cheery coal fire burned in the hearth. Although the house was centrally heated, on cold nights it was nice to have the comfort of an open fire.

My father told us all about the siege of Hong Kong and how he and my mother had been separated for three months after the war had started, with no news of each other. All that they now owned were the few clothes that they carried with them. As soon as the bombs started dropping, Mum had reported for nursing duty and was stationed at the Peninsular Hotel which had been turned into a military hospital. The hotel kitchen became an operating theatre. With a grave shortage of medical instruments, emergency operations were carried out on a food preparation table, using whatever kitchen utensils or carpentry tools that could be found. Mum had been on theatre duty one night when a Canadian soldier had had his leg amputated. There was no anaesthetic. The young soldier lay silent as the surgeon trimmed back the flesh with a carving knife. As he started to cut through the bone with a carpenter's saw, Mum fainted. The young soldier endured the ordeal without a murmur.

For several years before the Japanese attack, the 'top brass' of the British armed services had been accommodated at the Peninsular Hotel. These high ranking officers had their shaves and haircuts in the hotel barber shop by the little Japanese barber who had been there for ages and ages. He could barely string two words of English together so the officers freely discussed all sorts of delicate issues within his hearing. On the morning of 8 December 1941 the barber donned the uniform of a colonel in Japanese Intelligence. He had been educated at Oxford University and, needless to state, spoke faultless English.

He ordered that large Red Cross flags be made from hotel sheets and that they be flown from the hotel's flagpoles. Once they were in place, the heavy guns of the Japanese artillery were trundled into the quadrangle in front of the hotel and under the protection of the Red Cross flags they set about shelling Hong Kong. This deafening barrage went on day and night until the island's surrender on Christmas Day.

During a lull in the bombardment Mum had a visit from her amah who offered to accompany her to their apartment to rescue some personal belongings. They arrived to find the place had already been ransacked, but as they sorted through the mess for anything of value, some Japanese soldiers arrived on the scene and began helping themselves to what Mum and the amah had put aside. One stuck a bayonet through a picture of my sister as a baby. The amah started to object but Mum persuaded her that it would be wiser to neither protest nor remain. They left empty handed.

On the morning of 8 December, Dad had gone over to Hong Kong by ferry to attend language school. He was fluent in Mandarin but was brushing up on his Cantonese. At nine o'clock the bombs started falling as the Japanese dive-bombers swooped on the island. Confident of an early retaliation by the RAF, Dad and his fellow students watched at the window of the school and waited for the British planes to take to the air and start the counter-attack. They waited, and waited, and waited... Britain was totally unprepared. All the fortifications of Hong Kong were targeted towards an invasion from the sea and the attack from the mainland was a total surprise.

When Mum was on night duty she'd watch from the upper-storey windows of the hotel as wave after wave of dive-bombers plastered the island with explosives, wondering if her husband had survived those relentless attacks.

After Hong Kong fell the Japanese sent Mum and all the other Allied personnel of Kowloon to Stanley internment camp as prisoners of war. Word had filtered through that the ship we kids were to catch had been sunk with no survivors and she had heard nothing of Dad so things were pretty bleak for her. With the arrival of each new intake of prisoners she'd watch and wait, then turn away disappointed again and again.

Throughout the siege of Hong Kong the supply lines to the island had been cut. Many thousands of Chinese refugees were caught with little food and no accommodation, so my father set up a chain of refugee camps and soup kitchens. After Hong Kong fell and all enemy nationals were systematically rounded up and sent to Stanley, whenever the Japs came to arrest him, Dad asked them who'd run the refugee camps if he was taken prisoner, so they left him to continue his work. For three months he resisted arrest in this way but finally he was marched off to Stanley with the last group of prisoners and reunited with my mother.

Shortly after Dad arrived at Stanley, the prisoners were lined up and their valuables including watches, wedding and engagement rings and other personal items of jewellery were confiscated. Showing remarkable presence of mind, Mum removed her wedding ring and watch and got Dad to do likewise. Then with their rings and watches concealed in her handkerchief, she proceeded to cough and sneeze. The Jap soldiers had a phobia about infection—everywhere they went they wore white gauze face masks to keep out the nasties—so they gave this coughing, sneezing, disease-ridden woman a very wide berth. They didn't search her, so she saved their only remaining treasures.

Uncle Dorthe asked all sorts of questions about the camp and the treatment the POWs had received but much of this was beyond me. There had been many atrocities in Hong Kong before they'd been put into Stanley. Dad told of a group of young men who had been compelled to dig a long pit and then, when their task was complete, the Japanese soldiers made them stand beside it and they were beheaded. They were buried in the pit that they had dug.

There was a severe shortage of food in Stanley Camp and most of the prisoners suffered from beri-beri and dysentery.

One day a command came through that the camp Commandant wished to see my father and mother on a matter of the gravest importance. They had no inkling of the reason for the summons but suspected that any summons from the Commandant could only mean trouble. With trepidation they set off for the interrogation.

To their surprise they were greeted cordially and taken across to the Commandant's house where there were more cordial greetings as they were offered tea. The Commandant told them how fortunate they were that the Emperor had seen fit to show such great kindness to them by having them in the camp for their own protection. He went on to explain that in truth the Japanese people had the best interests of the world at heart, that they intended only friendship and goodwill towards the people of the Pacific region and in particular the people of Australia. It was for this reason that my father had been selected to offer a great service to the Emperor and his fellow Australians. The people of Australia must be made to understand the great feeling of goodwill that the Japanese felt towards them and my father had been given the honour of conveying that special message. He would do regular radio broadcasts that would be beamed to Australia to persuade the Australian government and people of the purity of Japan's intentions towards them. He would tell them that as the Japanese forces advanced towards their shores, they should offer no resistance, but rather welcome the Japanese troops as friends and benefactors.

In return for this service, my parents would be released from the camp, returned to Shanghai and given a suite at the Palace Hotel where they could live out the rest of the war in luxury and be suitably rewarded by the Emperor after Japan's inevitable victory.

My father refused.

The Commandant was furious. He screamed and ranted, shouting that my father would do as he was told.

Again Dad refused.

The Commandant called for the guard. My parents were seized and dragged off to the guardhouse where the Commandant again demanded that his instructions be obeyed and threatened that if my father persisted in his stubborn refusal he would be shot.

Still my father refused.

He was beaten, then dragged outside where my mother, watching through a window, saw him stood up against a wall. A firing squad was lined up in front of him. An order was given, the rifles were raised.

For my mother a lifetime passed. Another order was given, she clenched her fists, closed her eyes and waited. An eternity. The silence was deafening, it went on and on. Finally she opened her eyes to see that the guards had lowered their rifles and my father was being dragged back to the guardhouse. Inside they beat him again as the Commandant repeatedly demanded that he obey. His face was blackened but through his burst and bleeding lips he again refused.

The Commandant again ordered that he be taken out and shot. Once more the firing squad raised their rifles and took aim. This time my mother determined that she would not look away. She held her breath and waited for the volley of shots. Again the eternity of silence, the barked command, the lowered rifles and my father was dragged in for another beating.

In spite of the Commandant's threats and the beatings, my father refused to comply, so yet again he was taken out before the firing squad knowing that it was only a matter of time before the Commandant's patience would be exhausted and the order given to fire. As the guards raised their rifles for the third time there was a disturbance at the guardhouse door. Word had got out about what was happening and an Australian woman from the camp who'd heard of the offer that the Commandant had made to my parents had come to volunteer for the job. It let the Commandant off the hook. He accepted the substitute, and after ordering that my father be beaten again, presumably for luck, ordered that my parents be returned to the camp. The volunteer left Stanley and it is presumed that she carried out her duties as required by the Japs. My father didn't see her again until after the war when she was arrested by the Allied forces when she stepped off a plane in Hong Kong. We later heard that she'd been shot as a traitor.

The stories went on and on, but it had been a big day and we'd eaten dinner sitting around a cosy fire. I must have dozed off during the talking because the next thing I remembered was waking in a strange bed in a strange room with a fire already burning in the hearth and my clothes spread out on the chair to warm.

Coming back to Shanghai was a bit like coming home: it didn't take long to settle into the lifestyle. The city had not yet been greatly disrupted by the war. We still had to wear arm bands and there were shortages of most things, especially food, but most businesses continued to function, as did the schools. The new year was just starting so I was soon into a cassock and surplice to take my place in the choir stalls of the cathedral and back into the school uniform. As head master, the Rev P. C. Mathews still ruled with a rod of iron. He insisted that 'manners maketh man', that what every boy needed was some 'gumption and toothpaste', stressing this point with a clip under the ear and asking 'have you no brains, boy?' We took the question to be rhetorical but when out of his earshot we'd reply, 'No, Sir, I'm following in father's footsteps'. Above all, PC scorned the 'aristocratic and energetic game of marbles', which was banned in the school precincts. We played cricket, saying 'Shot sir' and clapping when players on either side did well. In the winter we played 'footer' (soccer) and 'rugger'. Tackling in the latter sport was supposed to be good for character-building. Fighting in the school grounds was decidedly lower class and not on. Rather, we were encouraged to settle our grievances with a few rounds in the gym, 'putting on the gloves and having it out like men'. PC taught maths and Latin and if in a foul mood, which was not infrequently, he came into class brandishing his cane which he wielded with abandon. Most of us lived in dread of him and learnt little or nothing under his tutelage, but in spite of this we worshipped him and the discipline that he meted out which, although it was strict and immediate, was always scrupulously fair.

It seemed that the war was passing us by in Shanghai. We listened to the BBC news and heard of the Japanese advance through the Pacific and of German progress in Europe, but we were immune. A number of people who my parents knew had been taken to the Bridge Road and Haiphong Road camps where their treatment was reportedly very brutal. There seemed to be no rhyme or reason for the arrests. Soldiers would arrive, usually in the middle of the night, and whisk people away. News of them was scant but it was rumoured that their treatment was far from good. On one occasion Dad received a letter from a fellow missionary in Haiphong Road. It told of the marvellous treatment that they were receiving at the hands of the

Japanese, the wonderful food and the kindness of the guards. It concluded by saying: 'I want you to tell everybody about this. I want you to tell it to the soldiers, I want you to tell it to the sailors and the airmen.' Then, to be absolutely sure that the sarcasm of the message was not missed, he added the wartime saying that accompanied any statement totally beyond belief, 'Above all I want you to tell it to the marines!'

But wars have a habit of catching up with you. Early one morning a group of Japanese soldiers appeared at our door. We were presented with a proclamation—the Japs were very big on proclamations—informing us that as enemies of the Emperor we were required to report to the grounds of the Shanghai Cathedral in a week's time. We would each be allowed one case of personal belongings which would include our bed clothes, and anything else that we could carry. After their experience in Hong Kong my parents had been expecting this and had stocked up on what they knew would be essentials.

On the appointed day we collected our cases and were bidden a tearful farewell by our servants as we set off for the cathedral grounds, where hundreds of Allied civilians were assembling, all carrying their few possessions. Some had golf clubs, some tennis rackets or baseball bats. Most called out to each other good-naturedly about how long the 'show' would last. Most likely only a few weeks, they said, and then they'd be back to resume their interrupted lives. There was no way that this motley bunch of yellow Nips could hold out against the Allies, especially now that the Yanks were into the war, what? Might as well enjoy the holiday while it lasted, eh? What ho!

I recognised many of my fellow prisoners. I could see PC with his ministerial dog collar, stooped shoulders and pipe—PC was never without a pipe—and I hoped he wouldn't be coming to our camp. There were several of the boys from school and from the choir. I caught a glimpse of Sonny Rees. He was my best friend, we were in the same form. The Japs divided us into groups and each of us was given a number—mine was 14-36. The date was the 15th—the Ides of March.

After standing in the hot sun for what seemed like hours we were ordered to form into ranks. We were a mixed bunch: English, Canadians, Australians, Americans, Filipinos, White Russians who were married to Britishers, and a large number of Eurasians. The order was given, and, carrying our possessions, we were marched off in various directions. Our contingent headed for the Bund. The passenger ships *Rajputana* and *Conte Verdi* were on their sides in the Whang Poo, where their crews had scuttled them at the start of the war to keep them out of enemy hands. The river wasn't deep enough for them to sink so they lay like enormous beached whales their rusting hulls covered in barnacles.

We were taken to an ageing cargo vessel which was tied up alongside and herded down into the holds. It was stifling with so many people crammed below decks. We'd had no food or water since morning and of course the toilet facilities were inadequate. Many of the group were elderly and had suffered badly as a result of the demands of the day and the long march. Some of the men banged against the bulkheads demanding attention from the Japs. Eventually the door opened, letting in some much-needed fresh air, and after a lot of argument it was agreed that some rations would be sent down. Half an hour or so later the door again opened and a large cauldron of rice, some boiled fish and a kettle of warm tea were passed in. There wasn't enough to go around so it was shared on the basis of elderly folk first, followed by young children, women, older children and, finally, men. The supply was exhausted long before the last groups were served and while I was flattered to have been considered one of the older children, I would have been perfectly happy if, just this once, I had been mistaken for one of the younger ones.

Some time late into the night the throb of the engines increased and we felt the ship move away from the wharf and some breeze waft in through the portholes.

By morning we'd been under way for several hours and were allowed on deck. We were well out to sea and the coast was away off on the horizon. In fact we had entered the Yangtse Kiang River, which is so wide that it looks like the open sea. Towards mid-morning we were given some more rice and another pot of warm tea. This time the food was rationed more carefully and there was enough to go around.

Shortly after midday the engines slowed and the ship dropped anchor off Chin Kiang. Some flat open barges towed by an ancient, wheezing tug pulled up alongside our ship and the order was given for us to clamber down rope ladders onto the barges. This adventure was rather fun for we young ones, but terrifying for the ill and the elderly, desperately clinging to their belongings and trying to negotiate the swinging ropes. The Japanese soldiers insisted that everyone carry their own belongings and would not allow any assistance for those in difficulty. When a woman who was partially crippled slipped, one of our number rushed forward to help her and was instantly felled by a rabbit punch from one of the guards.

In seconds all the able-bodied men in the group surged towards the guard who raised his rifle. Other guards also went for their weapons and it seemed inevitable that a massacre would take place. An officer barked out an order. The weapons were lowered, the guards stood back and we were permitted to render what assistance was needed for members of the group.

When we were all on board, the tug got up steam and slowly headed off towards the entrance to the Grand Canal. Someone started singing 'Wish me Luck as You Wave me Goodbye' and soon we joined in.

We were going to need it.

CHAPTER 9

BESIDE THE GRAND CANAL

The Grand Canal is over 1100 miles long. Work was started on it during the rule of the Mongol Emperors, around 400 BC, but the main canal was built in the thirteenth century to provide a link for transporting grain between Peking and the sea. Our destination was Yang Chow, some fifty miles up the canal, the city where Marco Polo had once been governor.

The little tug puffed and grunted, shooting smoke rings into the clear blue sky, while its propellers churned up the muddy water as it strained to tow its heavy load northwards. There were about 150 of us crammed aboard eight barges. Along the canal, fruit trees were festooned with spring blossoms, daffodils waved in the gentle breeze and a cover of fresh green grass graced the sloping banks. Sitting in the warm sunshine we speculated on what the future held for us. One thing was certain, the war must shortly come to an end. Why else would the Japanese officer have ordered his troops to lower their weapons? He'd know that Japan was on the run and no doubt hoped we'd remember this small favour in the days of retribution that were soon to come. In spite of our hunger our spirits were rising. We sang some of the Great War songs: 'Pack up Your Troubles in your old Kitbag', 'There's a Long Long Trail A-winding', 'It's a Long Way to Tipperary'. The younger people gave renditions of songs made famous by Vera Lynn and Gracie Fields as well as those of the popular bands of Benny Goodman, Tommy Dorsey and Glenn Miller. We waved and called out to the crews of the other barges that carried their loads of wood, coal, vegetables or grain up and down the canal and to the coolies who toiled on the banks.

Close to evening, when our tug ceased its grunting and came to rest at a small wharf outside the city wall of Yang Chow, most of us were convinced that we'd be on our way back in a couple of weeks.

About twenty uniformed soldiers with gauze masks protecting their faces shouted orders, shoved, pushed and cuffed as they formed us into rows on the bank of the canal. We were counted and recounted until they were satisfied that we were all there, then marched through an archway of the city wall, along a narrow dusty road to be stopped outside a black-painted gate in a high grey brick wall. As the gate swung open on creaking hinges, we proceeded on through the entrance courtyard into a large compound with several small buildings adjoining the entry court. On our right was a much larger grey brick building built in classic Chinese style, capped by a red terracotta tiled roof with green tiled dragons at each end of its ridge. It had the sloping rows of tiles with a traditional upward sweep to deflect airborne spirits and a lion face glowered menacingly at the end of each row.

We marched on around a grove of pine trees, past some giant poplars all of forty feet tall and sprouting their new spring growth. We were halted in front of a two-storey house that overlooked what looked like a playing field. It was clear that we weren't the first intake of prisoners, for standing in groups on the other side of the playing field were other POWs watching our arrival with considerable interest. One of them called out: 'Be careful. Watch your P's and Q's. The little Nips aren't fooling.'

One of our guards detached himself from our group and ran across the playing field, his right hand holding his cloth cap to his head, his left hand trying to control the erratic swinging of his enormous sword which seemed hell-bent on tripping him up. He looked so comical that many of us started to laugh. This goaded the rest of our guards into a fury of action, punching, kicking, cuffing. You have to experience the tooth-rattling force of a cuff by the gloved hand of a Japanese soldier to fully appreciate its effect. Well directed, it can easily fell a strong man.

Order and silence were quickly restored and we were called to attention and ordered to bow as the camp Commandant, Tanaka, mounted the steps and gave us a lecture in Japanese which was translated by an interpreter. We were told that, by the Emperor Hirohito's command and at great expense to the Japanese nation, we had been brought here to this Civil Assembly Centre for our own protection. That at the end of the war, when Japan had demonstrated her superiority by subduing all her adversaries, we would be required to repay the full cost of our accommodation and keep. This was the Yang Chow Civil Assembly Centre 'C' (from this we gleaned that somewhere in Yang Chow there must also be a Civil Assembly Centre 'A' and a Civil Assembly Centre 'B'). There was lots more posturing, but all we remembered was the gall of the man. Taking us prisoner and expecting us to meet the costs!

When Tanaka had finished we were again ordered to bow as he strutted off. A tall well-built man with grey hair and wearing a floppy straw hat mounted the steps. His top lip was covered by a large bushy white moustache. Introducing himself as Geordie Grant, he told us that he had been elected by the earlier arrivals to be the camp's Representative. It was his responsibility to act as intermediary between us and the Japanese. He understood how we felt at that moment, especially with regard to the charge for our keep, but pleaded with us to give him our full cooperation and to do nothing that might inflame the Japs unnecessarily. While they had the upper hand it would be unwise to goad them unduly. He gave us a run-down on the camp's rules then asked us to file past a long trestle table which had been set up under a large walnut tree where we were issued with ration cards and told where we'd be billeted. Our family were allocated beds in room 11 of house 3. We were shown a small sketch plan of the camp and a list of the camp rules. We were exhorted to abide by those rules for our own sakes as well as the sakes of the other inmates, as the guards had proven to be very unpredictable and could be vicious when provoked.

We had no difficulty finding house 3 and located room 11 which was to be our home for the next two and a half years. A medium size room about twenty foot by fifteen on the rear corner of the building, it had two outward-opening windows on the north and east. We had to share the room with three other families, fifteen people in all. Each person was allocated a space just large enough for their bed and a small trunk. The room had been curtained off into small sections giving, the present tenants some privacy. We were grateful that they had left us an area that included one of the windows. When all the beds were erected there was no space left to move about the room.

Our fellow room mates proved to be:

Mr and Mrs Savage with two sons and a daughter in their late teens. Mr Savage was an architect and his eldest boy had been training to become an engineer. The daughter was like a stereotyped nineteenth-century spinster. She dressed very plainly, wore no make-up of any kind and had her hair in two plaits curled into tight buns which she pinned just behind her ears.

Mrs Major Walker, with her teenaged son and daughter, had arrived as part of our contingent. Her husband was being held at Haiphong Road prison in Shanghai.

An elderly couple, both probably well into their sixties, whose name I can't recall, were to join us later. The husband was almost totally blind. He was a little man with grey hair, wore thick-lensed horn-rimmed glasses and smoked a Sherlock Holmes style pipe constantly. He was very good at chess and spent most of his time crouched over a chessboard with four-inch-high pieces, peering at them intently to identify them. I think he'd been involved in shipping before his retirement.

The Savages gave us a bit of a run down of camp life. The day started with a wake up call at 6.30. The breakfast queue usually started to form at around 7.00 outside the entrance to the dining hall and the breakfast ration was doled out at 7.30. You supplied your own food container and at all meals you needed your ration card to get served.

At 8.30 a.m. all prisoners had to form up on the playing field in house and room order to be counted.

The tiffin bell went at 12.30, supper was at 6 and we had to be in our rooms by 8.30 p.m. for the night roll call.

Lights out was at 9.00 p.m.

There was no running water in the camp but there were three wells in the compound and a communal bath house. The water was rationed out at half a bucket of cold water and one small thermos flask of boiling water per person per day. The shortage of food was the main problem, so talk about rations was the camp's major obsession.

The internal running of the camp was left to the inmates, a Camp Committee had been elected as a governing body to establish some sort of order in the community. The committee had allocated jobs and work rosters for the internees to staff the kitchen, bakehouse, PWD (public works department) and so on. There were three doctors who had brought with them as much medical equipment as they could carry. They had been billeted together in House 1, a section of which they had turned into a hospital.

The lecture we'd just received from Tanaka had been outside house 2. Behind us was house 3A which, being three storeys high, was the largest building in the camp. Its main advantage was that the rooms were small, so families didn't have to share. House 4 backed onto the kitchen and was near the dining hall. We'd actually come in by the side gate, they told us. There was a guardhouse and Tanaka's residence at the front gate. Before the war, the camp had been a missionary school compound. The large building we'd passed as we entered the camp was the bathhouse. It was divided into shower cubicles with duckboards on the floor. It had all the necessary plumbing fittings but with no reticulated water in the camp it could not serve the purpose for which it seemed to have been built, even if there hadn't been any water restrictions. There were two laundries near the kitchen that were used by men and women for personal bathing. With a ration of half a bucket of water per day, personal ablutions had to be kept to a minimum. The raw food rations were sent in weekly and controlled by the camp quartermaster who doled out the prescribed quantities to be prepared by the camp cooks for each meal.

As we talked the supper bell sounded so they helped us find our ration cards amongst the bits and pieces we had been handed when we arrived and aluminium pannikins in hand we set off to join the supper queue. From a grove of ash trees between the dining hall and the bathhouse a colony of rooks were swooping, cawing and soaring before settling down for the night.

There were just over 600 internees in the camp and the food ration was a small bowl of rice—about a cup and a half—a small turnip or two, some form of green vegetable—usually Chinese cabbage—and about a quarter of a loaf of bread per person per day, doled out at breakfast time. The meat ration was two ounces of pork per person per week.

Once we reached the head of the queue we presented our ration cards to be marked. First a serve of boiled rice was plonked into our pannikins then a ladle of liquid stew was poured over it. The stew had been made by boiling up all the day's rations in huge copper cauldrons in the camp kitchen. There wasn't much food, but as we hadn't eaten since breakfast it was very welcome and tasty enough.

Apparently the 'dining room' was used as an auditorium and most people ate their meals in their rooms. After the meal we unpacked our cases and set up our beds. By then it was rollcall time. We had to stand beside our beds while our house representative came around to each room accompanied by two Japanese guards. On the order 'Tootskay' we were required to come to attention, bow deeply and answer to our names. As the guards were not very strong on arithmetic it took several attempts before all of us were accounted for. Finally, when all was present and correct they moved on to the next room where the procedure was repeated. We had to remain by our bedsides until a bell was sounded indicating that the count for the house was correct. Talking during rollcall was forbidden.

It seemed that rollcall was barely over when the lights-out bell sounded and five minutes later the camp was plunged into darkness. We sat on the side of our iron bedsteads and chatted for a short time in undertones, conscious of the nearness of the other families in the room and trying not to overhear their attempts at private conversation. Then it was time turn in. It had been a long exhausting day but sleep seemed impossible. I was still hungry. The supper we'd just had only made me feel hungrier; the rice with the very liquid stew poured over it was more like a thick warm drink than a meal. How long were we going to be here, I wondered. Days? Months? Years?

I lay down on my bed, a rickety iron bedstead with unyielding steel springs over which was spread an uncomfortable, lumpy straw palliasse-type mattress that smelt musty. I could make out the shape of a mosquito net, tied in a large knot that hung down from the ceiling and, as the night crept slowly on, heard the sonorous breathing of the people on the other side of the curtained partitions.

And then the wake-up bell was sounding.

CHAPTER 10

YANG CHOW CAC "C"

It was morning. The camp was coming to life and although the sun was not yet up, the clear notes of a blackbird's song on the air was promise that it would be a beautiful spring day. I dressed quickly, splashed some icy water over my face from the large karng in the yard outside our window, collected our ration cards and the aluminium pannikins that we called tiffin-carriers and ran to join the breakfast queue. I was famished and wanted to be served first.

To my surprise I found that there were at least a hundred in the queue before me. The line moved so slowly that I was certain I'd starve to death before I reached the long, serving tables. At last it was my turn, a tick on the ration cards, a couple of ladles of warm, watery rice and five small pieces of bread. Was that all? I could have eaten twice that quantity on my own, but that was it—that was the morning ration for the five of us.

I hurried back to our room, careful not to spill a drop of the precious swill. Dad had packed up two of our beds, giving us a place to sit. I tucked in. A few small spoonfuls and the meal was over. It was warm and the bread was fresh and tasted good, but I couldn't imagine how I could go all day feeling this hungry.

After breakfast I took our tiffin-carriers to the communal wash-up area just outside the kitchen. Nearby were large bamboo 'slop buckets' into which any unwanted food scraps were scraped. From the look of them, the buckets were well-named, but I couldn't imagine anyone having enough food to be able to throw any away. Standing on a trestle table were two more bamboo buckets filled with tepid washing-up water which was covered with a scum of yellow oil that clung to your hands leaving them feeling clammy. It was impossible to get the pannikins properly clean but I did the best

I could, wiped them on the tea-towel that I'd brought with me and took them back to our room. Shortly after I got back, the rollcall bell sounded for us to form up in rows on the parade ground.

About twenty minutes later the Jap guards marched across from the guardhouse wearing black uniforms and black cloth caps, their enormous swords swinging and clanking by their sides. Some of them wore mauser weapons. They stopped in front of the first row and an order was shouted in Japanese—'Tootskay'

'Attention!' the interpreter called.

'Bungo!' shouted the head guard.

'Number!' ordered the interpreter, and down the line it went. 'One, two, three, four . . .' and so on to the end of the line. The count was checked against a list then another order was given.

'Smet!'

'At ease!' called the interpreter and the group moved on to the second row.

In our row the count didn't match the tally sheet so we had to number off again, and yet again. The guards were becoming belligerent and tempers started to fray until Geordie Grant came over. A hurried discussion took place.

'Ah so, ah so. Sodeska,' said the head guard and burst into laughter. The tally list had not taken into account our arrival at the camp.

When we were dismissed I set off to explore the camp. There were quite a number of boys I knew from school and they showed me around, introducing me to some of the other boys, many of whom were Eurasians who carried British citizenship. There were also quite a few Filipinos. The main attraction seemed to be the piggery – there weren't any pigs, but for a few months there were half a dozen goats that supplied a little milk for use in the hospital. It was a rambling place with about a dozen stone-built sties that we clambered all over. In amongst the stones were pieces of coloured pottery that we were sure must have belonged to Marco Polo.

Another fascination was the trees and birdlife, especially in the huge poplars, where giant kites with wingspans of over six feet, had built their ragged nests of interwoven sticks. Smaller birds used the heavy sticks surrounding the kites' nests to anchor their nests of straw and small twigs. They seemed to live quite happily under the eye of the kites. We were enraptured by the 'kreeee' call of the kites as they spiralled higher and higher on motionless pinions. We'd watch in awe as they'd plummet down in full stoop on some hapless rodent, grasping it in their powerful talons. Then laboriously beating their mighty wings, they'd carry their prey up to the chicks in their nests. Flights of rooks rose from the rookeries in the groves of ash and elm trees and the rows of cyprus trees between houses 1 and 2 were home for bullfinches, bulbuls, shrikes and several varieties of tit. Like miniature pneumatic drills, woodpeckers hammered away at tree trunks; magpies, blackbirds, larks and blue jays, as well as rock and turtle doves, strutted on the parade ground while sparrowhawks, harriers and falcons flashed through the treetops. It was a bird fancier's paradise.

Excitedly we rushed about the grounds picking up feathers, trying to identify the birds they came from. One of the boys said his father was an 'orthinologist' so he knew all about birds and their nests and how to suck birds' eggs. I didn't know what an 'orthinologist' was but it sounded like a pretty good thing to be and I decided that I'd like to be one when I grew up.

Near the main gate and encompassed by a paved pathway were the guardhouse and Tanaka's residence. All this area was out of bounds to prisoners. Around Tanaka's place was another grove of pines where the guards set fowlers nets to catch small birds to supplement their diet. If we got to the netted birds before the Nips, we'd try to save them. Our attempts were often futile as the poor little birds' necks were broken.

Close by the guardhouse and on the in-bounds side of the pathway was the church, the back half of which had been curtained off to accommodate about fifty people. Both the Catholics and Protestants used the front part on Sundays; they'd come to an agreement to alternate their morning and evening services, so that one month the Catholics would have the morning and the Protestants the evening service, then the following month it would be the other way about. A little way from the church was a tiny enclosed courtyard which was to become the cemetery. Down from the church, on the western side of the grounds, the houses moved down more or less in a row, 1, 2 and 3. House 3A was a long narrow building behind house 3. It stretched almost the whole width of the compound, stopping just short of the laundry which was against the eastern wall. In front of the east end of 3A was house 4 in the shape of a quadrangle.

Behind house 2, and built against the west wall, were a series of small buildings that were used by the camp's PWD to store their tools for maintenance work around the compound. One of these sheds was being operated by a Chinese trader as a shop which sold, at highly inflated prices, essentials such as dishes, cutlery, thermos flasks, tea, some items of clothing and, very occasionally, cigarettes. Most of the internees had brought some money into the camp with them, so they were able to take advantage of the items offered by this entrepreneurial trader. Among the food items was a kind of spread called mizuami, which I think was a mixture of ground sesame seed and soya been. The main items of clothing were corduroy ski-type suits which were referred to as cod-liver oil suits because of their colour. They had a pink fleecy lining. The store functioned for a couple of months and helped to supplement the camp rations until the prisoner's supply of money ran out.

After food, cigarettes were the most sought-after commodity. Supplies were running very low and there weren't enough to go around. Butts were kept and the tobacco recycled. When the supply of tobacco dwindled, smokers used dried tea-leaves wrapped in toilet paper. Apparently the paper didn't taste too good so most men whittled themselves wooden pipes from branches cut off a couple of old cherry trees.

Near the bathhouse was a boiler room with a couple of large copper cauldrons where the water was boiled and tipped into five-gallon bamboo buckets with wooden dowel handles. The men on boiling water duty would carry these buckets two at a time from the boiler room to the kitchen, shouting 'Gangway, boiling water!'

Each morning we queued at the boiler room, thermos flasks in hand, for our daily ration of hot water—one flask per adult, half a flask per child.

Apart from the small quantity of rainwater that was caught in the karngs outside each of the houses, the camp's water supply was reliant on three wells, one behind the hospital, one outside house 2 and one in front of the house 4 quadrangle. All were equipped with hand-operated suction pumps that were manned by the men on pump duty. After rollcall we queued, ration cards in hand, for our daily quota of half a bucket of water per person. The pumps had to be primed each morning because their leather washers lost suction when they dried.

Christmas carolling, 1941. I am in the front.

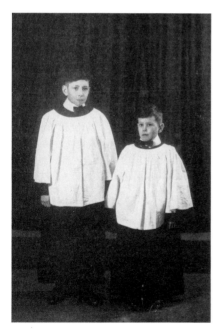

My elder brother and I were choir boys
in the Holy Trinity Cathedral, Shanghai.

No. 8 Yang Terrace where we lived in
Shanghai.

Train passengers even clung precariously to the roof.

The block of flats at Kowloon where we stayed after being evacuated from Shanghai.

My class on top of the bakehouse woodpile. *Clockwise from top left:* Kenneth Gibson, Leslie 'Goo Goo' Green, Jimmy Gittens, David Derrick Dennis Denton, unknown, Neil Begley, David Bolton, Peter Gibson, Joey Azachee (squatting), Walford Gillison, Wally Atkinson, Cyril Mack, ? da Silva

House 4. About 140 people were accommodated here.

Above and below: queuing for Yang Chow Stew.

The Camp Church.

The bakehouse staff. My father is third from the right.

A group of POWs outside the hospital.

The butchers at work.

Hanging from a spreading oak tree between houses 2 and 3 was a large bronze bell which was rung to announce the important events of the day: wake-up time, breakfast, rollcall parade, tiffin, supper, evening rollcall and lights-out. It would also be rung for emergencies such as fires.

Our toilet facilities were pretty basic. Behind each house were two long toilet blocks with twenty or so cubicles each containing a rough-hewn toilet seat over a bamboo bucket. On the wall of each cubicle was a nail from which hung sheets of Clo Pah a coarse-grained toilet paper. Once a week we had a visit from the mordung amahs, Chinese ladies who came into the camp to empty the buckets into large bamboo barrels mounted on wheelbarrows. The contents were used to fertilise their crops.

It was about half a mile around the perimeter of the camp where there was a well-trodden track that you'd walk when you needed to be alone, or if you needed company, or you needed to think, or you couldn't bear to think any more. Inmates would walk round and round, singly, in pairs or in groups, hour after hour, day after day. It was the major camp occupation. Some folk played bridge, some chess, some played board games like Monopoly, or sat around and yarned, but everyone walked.

In spite of all the distractions of the camp grounds we were always hungry. Conversation kept turning to food. How long was it to tiffin time? Did you get used to being hungry all the time? Surely the rations would be increased as soon as the Nips realised how many of us there were in the camp. At about 11.30 it was time to join the tiffin queue. Thank goodness! We ran back to our rooms, collected our tiffin carriers and ration cards and took our places in the line. This would be the pattern for the duration of our internment—queues, queues and still more queues, and all for a measly serve of what in time became a barely edible slush. The stew varied with the season. In addition to our rice ration we got some vegetables. In the summer these comprised large, old and tasteless carrots and rather tired leaves of Chinese cabbage. When carrots went out of season they were replaced by rather woody turnips. However, in the early part of camp life the bread was good, especially when it was fresh and hot. The Japs supplied us with white flour and yeast and the camp bakers did a creditable job. Unfortunately if you saved some of your ration to have next day it was a bit stale.

For the first few months we were left pretty well to our own devices and, apart from the occasional beating, nothing untoward happened. Anyway, most of the POWs weren't too concerned, they were certain that our stay at Yang Chow would be a bit like a short summer holiday. Before long they'd be on their way back to Shanghai, where they'd resume their business pursuits after what was little more than a minor inconvenience. Instead of winter clothing, many had brought sporting equipment with them, so although the shortage of food was taking its toll, most of us combated that with plenty of outdoors activity. After the cricket pitch was set up, softball and baseball diamonds were marked out on the parade ground and we soon learnt how to 'peg' a ball and catch it with a softball glove, how to hit with a round bat and steal bases. Most of us youngsters were having a wonderful time. It was like living at a holiday camp.

But not all of us could take part the sports. There was Yalli Wah, a Eurasian boy of about eleven who was deaf and almost mute. We had no idea what his real name was but we called him 'Yalli Wah' because these were the only words he could speak. When he was younger he'd fallen and been impaled through the nose by a steel spike. As a result his nose was now three blobs on the front of his face, separated by a single nostril. Although he couldn't hear and the only sounds he could utter were 'Yalli Wah', we soon learnt to converse with him by means of an improvised sign language. There was Billy Spencer, who had the most horribly twisted legs that I had seen. I think he was twelve or thirteen. Somehow he dragged himself around using a pair of sticks, walking, if you could call it that, on the sides of his feet. His disability seemed to do little to prevent him from finding his way around the camp, but although he was remarkably cheerful, he had to be a loner. With the cruelty that is so characteristic of groups of children, we excluded him from most of our activities.

Then there was 'Slop Bucket.' His real name was John, but like many Johns in China at that time he was called 'Sonny'. When he went into the camp he was fat, ungainly and dreadfully untidy. He always seemed to have a cold. Two revolting strings of snot would hang from his nostrils and extend down getting longer and longer like strips of yellow/green spaghetti until, just when you thought the force of gravity must take over, he'd inhale with a disgusting snort and suck them back into his nose. The process would be repeated again and again. Not surprisingly, Slop wasn't one of the most popular boys in the camp especially in winter. In the early days his bulk made him an unlikely participant in most sports. The risks involved in a full faced collision with him when he had a cold made us wary of selecting him for body-contact sports like baseball, soccer or rugby.

There were heaps of kids, probably over a hundred in all, and we very quickly adapted to camp life. Although hunger was always there, with summer coming on it looked as if we'd have a pretty good time, and we set about to enjoy ourselves.

Joey Azachee was the King of the Kids. A born leader, Joey soon established his position, which was accepted with few attempts to challenge it. Although he was only about twelve, Joey was a real street kid, tough and experienced beyond anything we dreamed of. Somehow he'd smuggled a switch knife into the camp which we had no doubt he'd use on anyone who crossed him. He had a swarthy complexion, with piercing dark brown eyes set too close together astride a prominent beak-like nose. He had a long body and rather short legs which were slightly bowed. He wore his jet black hair slicked back and had the assurance of someone twice his age. Joey said his father was Japanese but his parents had separated, and as his mother was British they'd ended up in the camp with the rest of us.

Joey would entertain us for hours telling us movies he had seen or stories that he made up as he went along. He'd act out the various parts and change his voice to suit the characters. He'd seen all of Mickey Rooney's movies, knew about Beau Geste and the Three Musketeers and D'Artagnon. He'd been to the Canadrome, which was Shanghai's greyhound racing stadium, and he'd watched jai a lai, reputed to be one of the fastest games in the world. Joey wasn't much for sport himself but he was a past master at marbles and seldom lost a contest, even if he had to change the rules mid-game to achieve this end.

He'd done everything and been everywhere, even to Harbin. On one occasion I timorously mentioned that I had been to Australia, several of the Pacific Islands and Japan, but Joey pointed out scornfully that that was nothing alongside having been to Harbin, which was full of gambling casinos, brothels and incredibly beautiful women.

We found a trapdoor under the dining hall and about a dozen of us used to congregate in the semi darkness under the floor boards, hanging on Joey's every utterance. He told us that he had been a member of one of Shanghai's most notorious street gangs and that his gang would wait around outside the brothels to watch the American Marines go in to do something he called rooting. When they came out, he told us, they'd walk with a curious stiff-legged gait which he tried to demonstrate in the confined space of our hide-out. 'That's how men walk after they've done rooting.' he told us. After they'd been rooting they couldn't run away, which made their wallets easy prey for the gang.

He also told us about the various parts of the female anatomy and taught us how to take out our 'pricks' and rub them until they got hard and then to keep going until we couldn't stand the sensation any longer. He told us that when we got older, spunk would come out. He'd seen men do this often and that the spunk was black. It was called 'tossing off', he said.

My parents urged me to keep away from Joey because he wasn't a nice boy, but nice boy or no, nothing would have kept me from those rendezvous under the dining hall.

CHAPTER 11

BACK TO SCHOOL

B efore we'd come into the camp, things had been going pretty
well for Japan in the Pacific arena. Their advance down to Malaya
and Singapore and on through the Philippines had given them a
string of easy victories. They had the Allies on the run and seemed
certain to conquer the South Pacific Islands, Australia and New
Zealand. Their successes were confirmed by the reports that we read
from the newspapers they sent into the camp every month or so. As
we'd only get one copy of each paper, it would be pinned up on the
noticeboard near the bathhouse. Starved of news from the outside
world, we'd gather around, jockeying for position to read every
word. The papers were full of Japanese propaganda, but even allowing
for that the news was all bad. We lost count of the times that the Jap
Navy had sunk the total Allied fleet and their army had wiped out
all our land bases, but the fact remained that the Nips had advanced
south, through the Marshalls, New Guinea, the Gilberts,
Guadalcanal, and that Australia was at risk. Any chance of an early
Allied victory seemed to be getting rather remote—in fact very remote
indeed. Although we were confident that the British Empire was
invincible, we wondered how effective her counter-attack was
proving to be.

If the Nips believed their own propaganda they could afford to
be magnanimous, but in spite of this, with a bit of sake to urge them
on, they periodically dealt out some rather horrible beatings. We
often wondered if they considered this a form of sport or exercise as
there seemed no obvious reason for the attacks. As children we
escaped much of the brutality, but adults seemed to be fair game.
One chap in particular was often singled out for particularly brutal
treatment. He had lived in Japan for many years where he had been

101

decorated by the Emperor. He spoke fluent Japanese and considered the guards his inferiors, addressing them as such. They took exception to his manner retaliating in the best way they knew how, with violence.

Predictably, the camp had its share of spies—prisoners who would sneak over to the guardhouse after lights-out and, in return for a few favours, a packet of cigarettes or some extra rations, rat on their fellow internees. We soon learnt who the pimps were but it was impossible to exclude them from everything that went on in the camp and frequently they would pick up gossip of a planned escape or an attempt to build a radio. This information would be relayed to the Japs, who'd carry out surprise searches of our quarters. Beds would be overturned, floorboards pulled up, improvised cupboards wrecked in search of evidence, and suspects beaten or taken away to the guardhouse for further interrogation. They'd return bruised and bleeding.

In spite of everything, life wasn't all that bad. We craved more food and the smokers, who comprised some of the women and most of the men, were really suffering for want of sufficient tobacco. When the tea-leaves ran out they tried all sorts of improvisations. For a short while they got some corn silk from the mordung amahs, but that supply soon dried up also. Wicker chairs weren't safe, bits of the wicker cane would be broken off, lit and smoked. Pretty well every kind of herb was dried and tried in the cherrywood pipes.

Added to the shortage of tobacco was the scarcity of matches, so magnifying glasses and lenses of any sort were used to concentrate the sun's rays onto the contents of a pipe until a faint stream of silver-grey smoke wafted upwards. This was coaxed into a red glow until, with careful sucking, the pipe was going at full blast, but it wasn't easy to start a pipe on a cloudy, rainy day. The words of 'Pack up Your Troubles in Your Old Kit Bag' were changed from 'While you've a lucifer to light your fag . . .' to 'While you've a burning glass to light your pipe, smile boys that's the style . . .'

Another major shortage was razor blades. With a tiny ration of hot water, little soap and very blunt razor blades, shaving wasn't much fun. But it was considered very poor form to go unshaven, in fact it was the first sign that a man was losing his grip, and patriotism demanded that we'd die before we let the Nips think that they were wearing us down. We were British! So every morning the men scratched and scraped at their faces, nicking out lumps of flesh. Then they'd carefully rehone the razor blades for another day. Some stropped the blades on leather belts, some on the soles of shoes, some on very smooth fine stone. My dad had a small mechanical device with a pull cord that sharpened both sides of a razor blade at the same time and he'd often touch up a batch of blades to keep the camp supply going. From his experience in Stanley Camp he guessed that there would be the need for a shoemaker so while in Shanghai he'd stocked up with twine, pigs' bristles, awls, knives and beeswax. With these items he set up as the camp cobbler, doing running repairs to footballs, softballs, and cricket balls as well as worn-out shoes which he was able to repair with some old car tyres that had been found in the camp store.

There was also a serious shortage of clothing. Many of the prisoners, sure that the war would be over in a few weeks, had brought few clothes with them. As their plight became desperate flour bags were cut down and resewn as shirts, blouses and underwear.

Rather like a parliament, elections for the Camp Committee took place from time to time, I can't recall how frequently but they were probably held annually. They were taken very seriously and vigorously contested with the candidates running election campaigns. On the appointed day, ballot boxes, supervised by scrutineers, were set up in the dining hall. As in the outside world, all persons over the age of twenty-one were entitled to vote and after the count the results were posted on the notice board at the dining hall door.

The Camp Committee did its best to make our enforced community living as pleasant as circumstances would allow. In an attempt to preserve the extraordinary variety of the camp's birdlife, the committee passed a rule that disturbing birds at nesting time was forbidden, but that didn't stop us. Bird-nesting was a popular hobby. In the very early mornings while the adults still slept and the air was filled with the calls of courting doves, the cry of cuckoos and the liquid warblings of golden orioles, we'd sneak out from our rooms into the spring semi-light to climb trees and rob the nests where we'd observed birds setting during the day. We imposed our own rule that you never took more than one egg from a nest, but that didn't limit the number of boys who each took an egg from the same nest. We'd drill a tiny hole in each end of the egg and blow out the contents. As we became more skilful we perfected the art of blowing an egg with only one hole. We also learnt that if an unblown egg floated in water it was addled; a chick had started to hatch and the egg couldn't be blown. Many of us built up quite extensive collections, but no one had a kite's egg. We didn't dare climb to the top of the giant poplars where the kites nested.

The Chinese pastime of cricket fighting was another popular activity for us. We'd catch male fighting crickets—the females don't fight; we could tell the difference because male crickets have two tails while the females have three—and keep them in cages that we made from pieces of bamboo with tiny bars to give them ventilation. We fed them on grains of boiled rice that we saved from our meals. To train them we'd tease them with ticklers that we made by splitting fine stems of grass. The crickets would mistake the ticklers for the antlers of other crickets and attack the grass. When our charges had become sufficiently aggressive we'd place two of them in a bowl that we'd fashioned from clay and coax them around with the ticklers until their feelers touched. They'd then set upon each other with opened jaws and fight until one surrendered and ran away. The victor would spread his wings and chirp his victory song.

We also played marbles and tops—both very popular games amongst children in China. Our tops were made from turned wood, more or less egg-shaped with a pointed steel cap at the bottom and a round knob at the top. By wrapping a piece of cord around the top and throwing it at the ground we could whip it into a spin. We had top fights trying to split an opponent's top with the steel cap of your own.

There were two major games of marbles, one was five holes, where we set out an area about six feet square with a three-inch-diameter hole on each corner and one in the middle. We'd bet marbles on our skill and, aiming in turn, the first player to get around the course and into the centre hole was the winner. You had to run the gauntlet of the other players trying to 'sting' your marble away if they got close to you.

The other game was hit-ya-gets. The owner of a prized marble like a 'puree' or an unchipped 'agate' or even a good 'stoney' would place it on a clear piece of ground, draw a line about twelve or fifteen feet away, and invite all comers to aim from the line at the prize. If you hit it you got to keep it. All marbles that missed became the property of the kid running the game. Your wealth in marbles varied with your skill and a fair degree of luck. 'Fudging' was not allowed. All shots had to be from the line in hit-ya-gets, or from where your marble rested in five holes, and the aiming hand had to be absolutely still when firing. Marbles was a serious business for us and we all knew who owned the rare and sought-after marbles.

'Parcels! Parcels!' the cry went round the camp. People were running towards the guardhouse calling 'Parcels'. Outside the guardhouse a lorry was unloading cardboard cartons with large red crosses emblazoned on their sides. The Red Cross had found out where we were and sent in some food. The guards made us stand back until the lorry was unloaded, then as it drove away we watched in disbelief as they opened the cartons and helped themselves to what they wanted. We got what was left. There were about forty parcels in all, containing powdered milk, tinned meat, jam, cigarettes, chocolates, razor blades and a few medications. After the Nips had helped themselves we ended up with about half the contents. The tinned milk, razor blades and cigarettes were treasures. Where possible, we were each given an equal ration of everything the parcels contained. Then a shop was set up where people could exchange what they didn't want for what they needed. A currency had to be arrived at so everything was valued, not in money, but in cigarettes. A can of milk may have been say 150 cigarettes, a small block of cheddar 80 cigarettes and a packet of razor blades 70. On this scale a block of cheese and a packet of razor blades could buy a can of milk. The system worked remarkably well and was the basis for all bartering in the camp for the rest of the war.

There was a large Chinese walnut tree and a couple of big pecan nut trees in the camp and when the nuts were ripe we boys would knock them down by throwing tennis balls at them. We soon got to be very accurate and could bring down a pecan nut from the top of a tree with four or five shots. We'd carefully cut the bottom off the nuts, remove and eat the kernel then drill holes in the top of the nut, polish it and add a small stopper to turn it into a salt or pepper shaker—not that we had either salt or pepper to put into the shaker.

The walnuts were inedible. We tried them but they made us sick, as did the seeds from the castor oil plants that were plentiful around the piggery, but the crushed husks from the outside of the walnuts produced a permanent stain the colour of iodine which we used to stain the carvings that we whittled with our small penknives. Yellow box, privet and cherrywood were greatly prized as carving timbers. Most of these shrubs had been cut out in the first months we were in the camp, but any remaining pieces were dried and carved into ornaments.

There were a couple of pomegranate and persimmon trees up near the guardhouse, but they were out of bounds. If we were feeling particularly brave or foolhardy—usually for a dare—we'd sneak up and raid them

The older boys—the term teenager had not yet been coined—formed themselves into a group called the Night Hawks which became rather like a service organisation. They undertook numerous projects and were always available where voluntary manpower was needed. We little kids were too small to be Night Hawks but, not to be outdone we formed ourselves into the Night Owls. Apart from meeting under the dining room I can't recall anything of moment that the Night Owls ever achieved. We'd spend our time devising the tortures we'd mete out to Hitler, Mussolini, Tojo and Hirohito after the war to say nothing of Tanaka. We'd suspend them over a nest of red ants, strung up by their thumbs with their toes just brushing the nest. With a sharp knife we'd then peel off their skin and cover their bodies with small cuts so the ants could feast on them with ease. Under Joey's tutelage we were developing into charming children.

We composed songs which we sang around the camp with great gusto if we thought there were no adults within ear shot. One was to the tune of Colonel Bogey:

Hitler has only got one ball,
Goering has got his two—both small.
Himmler
Is something sim'lar,

But poor old Goebbels
Has no b'lls
At all.
[*Repeat ad nauseam.*]

The others were 'beyond the pale'.

Understandably, our parents were becoming concerned at the way we were running wild. We followed Joey's lead in everything and it was futile for them to tell us that we shouldn't get mixed up with 'bad company'.

But Mr L. P. Quincy came to the rescue. He'd run a gymnasium in Shanghai so he started a gym in the camp to keep us boys fit. With the initials L.P.Q., behind his back we called him Low Pee Koo, Chinese for 'Old Back Side'. At five-thirty in the morning he'd assemble us in a corner of the camp grounds and put us through all sorts of physical training. We did arm, leg and stomach exercises. We did push-ups and chinned the bar on tree branches. To strengthen our stomach muscles we'd take turns sitting on a bench with someone holding our feet, then bend back until our heads touched the ground then forward to bring our heads between our knees. For dumbbells and weights we used bricks. In spite of our poor diet, we became surprisingly fit and very strong. He set us objectives then he forced us to attain them: 100 push-ups, 100 chins of the bar, 200 sit-ups. We took great pride in our muscles and had competitions, taking turns punching each other in the stomach to see how much punishment we could endure.

As luck would have it P. C. Mathews ended up in our camp and he too was concerned at the way most of us were turning out. We unhesitatingly acquired all the worst traits of the people we mixed with and didn't pick up too many good ones. It worried PC that we weren't getting a formal education, so he set about establishing a school. He was the only qualified male teacher in the camp and was faced with the challenge of about 100 potential delinquents or Shanghai mobsters. As the internees comprised a wide cross-section of the community; doctors, a dentist, an optician, a surveyor, a mountaineer, numerous missionaries, a couple of Catholic priests, a playwright, several professional musicians, a large smattering of public servants, a couple of policemen, accountants, a mathematician and many others, PC co-opted a staff from amongst this wealth of experience to help him with his project.

Two schools were formed—in true British tradition, there was a school for boys and one for the girls. Yes there were girls in the camp, plenty of them, but when you're ten going on eleven and in the thrall of someone like Joey Azachee, who's got time to worry about *girls*! At any rate our halcyon days of careless leisure were at an end. A curriculum was laid down and school hours set. We were divided into classes based on age, ability and availability of teachers.

Not surprisingly, there were a few problems to be overcome. The first was the absence of textbooks. Most of the volunteer teachers had to instruct entirely from memory. This was not a problem when it came to geography, which was taught by the mountaineer who'd been passing through China on his way to the Himalayas when the war broke out and who found himself in camp with us. There weren't many places in the world he hadn't been. He'd climbed the mountains he taught us about and crossed most of the rivers. His lessons were embellished by stories of adventure that kept us enthralled. The same was true of Mr Willis, who had been a surveyor before he became a missionary. He taught us maths, and to impress on us the importance of trigonometry, he recounted stories of his surveying days in the wilds of Canada where, if he encountered a frozen lake, he had the choice of breaking the ice and wading or swimming across with a tape measure tied around his waist, or calculating the distance using the help of Pythagoras and trigonometry. He told us that the Pythagoras theorem was known as Pons Assinorum, the asses' bridge, but he never made it entirely clear whether the asses were those who were halted by its complexity or those who succeeded in crossing over it. He also taught us physics and initiated us into the wonders of gravity, electricity and magnetism. He introduced us to classical Greek using the New Testament as his textbook. An accomplished, artist he drew us texts embellished with Olde Englishe type illuminations.

But the teacher I remember best was Father Thornton. He was an Irish/American Jesuit priest who couldn't pronounce 'th's so called himself 'Farder Tornton', and of course behind his back we did too. He had a passion for English literature and seemed to be able to recite from memory everything that Shakespeare had written, and Shelley, and Thomas Gray, and Coleridge, Milton, Keats and Tennyson, with a few others thrown in, and he tried to foster the same passion in us. He recited to us in chunks and we learnt it that way. We had to be able to quote Mark Anthony's speech over the body of Caesar; Tennyson's 'Brook' or Shelley's 'Skylark', Wordsworth's 'Daffodils and 'Upon Westminster Bridge'; Thomas Gray's 'Elegy Written in a Country Churchyard' and 'The Ancient Mariner' from beginning to end. They were all learnt, never to be forgotten and how grateful I am to him for the rich memory of those words that have kept me company through seemingly endless sleepless nights or on long trips or during times of quiet contemplation. He told us the stories of Kidnapped and Treasure Island and acted out the parts of Long John Silver or Ben Gunn or Davy Lad and made them come alive.

Not only were we without textbooks in our school but we were also without exercise books, or any writing paper for that matter, on which to take notes, so the Camp Committee issued an edict that no blank piece of paper was to be used for *any* purpose until it had been written on both sides. That released a whole supply of note paper. The Clo Pah from the toilets was used for short-term notes, then the written-on sheets were returned to the toilets for their intended purpose. In the case of subjects like Latin and classical Greek we put our notes to their final use with some sense of satisfaction.

All labels from the tins that came in Red Cross parcels were removed and bound into book form. These were used for recording long term information and for exams. PC kept these exams in the hope that Cambridge University would accept them after the war and credit the students with the results that had been attained in the camp.

As well as English, Maths, Science, Geography and Classical Greek, we learnt Physiology, History and French. In a further attempt to curb our wildness the teachers imposed strict discipline and masses of homework which of necessity was of a practical nature. In science, for instance, we had to make a suction pump using pieces of bamboo and marbles as valves. In spite of this the lure of the hide-out under the dining room and the crickets, tops and marbles occupied a lot of our free time much to the ire of PC. We lived in more fear of him than we did of the Japs. He used his cane with abandon and when you got 'six of the best' from PC you remembered it.

PC's application of the cane was not restricted to school misdemeanours. Transgression of camp rules could result in a visit to his room under the stairs. One camp rule said we were not allowed to throw tennis balls at the nuts in the pecan trees after the school assembly bell had sounded. There was one large nut at the top of a tree that had eluded all our attempts to dislodge it and I was determined that it should be mine. I was taking aim just as the bell sounded but nevertheless I let fly with a shot that was a direct hit and down came the nut. Well, that was the good part. A fussy old gentleman for whom I was never able to muster the highest respect, was witness to the offence. He sent a report in to PC and I got six of the best!

You'd have to report to his room, knock on the door then wait for the gruff, 'Come in'.

Warily you'd open the door of his tiny room which was not much more than a cupboard under the stairs. There was a bed against the longest wall, a small table which PC used for a desk and a straight-backed wooden chair. He'd be standing peering at you through his thick glasses, a pipe clamped in teeth that were cracked, twisted and stained brown from years of smoking. At the edges of his mouth small flecks of white saliva stretched and receded when he spoke. He was a little man, his shoulders were stooped and his cheek-bones poked out at you as if they, and his long hooked nose were trying to form a protective platform over the protruding teeth.

'Why are you here, boy? Speak up boy. Speak up like a man.'

Nervously, 'I was sent to see you Sir.'

'Do you know what you're here for boy . . . Well do you? Speak up boy, speak up!' the lips moved as he spoke but the teeth remained clamped firmly onto the pipe stem,

'Yes Sir.'

'You know you've broken the rules boy?'

'Yes Sir.'

'You know what the penalty is?'

'Yes Sir.'

'Well take it like a man. Bend down and touch your toes.'

Thanks to Mr Quincey's exercises that was easy enough—rumour had it that if you couldn't touch your toes it earned you an extra couple of cuts. Then PC checked your shorts for any sign of padding.

'Y'ready boy?'

'Yes Sir.'

There was the swish of the cane and the sting of the first cut. 'One' you'd count under your breath, biting your lips in case you let out a cry, 'two, three, four, five,' then finally 'six'.

It was over and you hadn't cracked.

'Stand up boy' PC was saying, 'stand up and rub it. Rub it boy. Get the circulation going that's the ticket'.

While you fought back the tears he'd go over to the little table and from his thermos pour out two precious rations of tea. Somehow, we never knew how, he'd conjure up a couple of biscuits, invite you to sit down on the bed and serve you a cup with one of the biscuits. He'd talk to you about general matters and then, when the tea was finished, dismiss you. As you headed for the door, he'd shake you firmly by the hand and say,

'You broke the rules boy, you've taken your punishment like a man. I'm proud of you boy. This will never be raised between us again.' And he meant it. As far as PC was concerned the slate was wiped clean.

Gradually he moulded us back to some form of the discipline that he'd imposed at the Cathedral School, and although he petrified us we all agreed that he was absolutely fair. If you got six of the best from PC you'd probably deserved it.

CHAPTER 12

GROWING UP

There was no shortage of entertainment in the camp. The professional actors, playwrights and musicians quickly formed themselves into a concert party. To keep up camp morale anyone who showed some interest was encouraged to join in . They wrote and performed songs and plays with a patriotic background. Songs that told of Britannia's might and England's glory. Their first show was a camp fire night which was held on the parade ground after dinner and before lights out. Many of us were pressed into service to sing or perform in some way or other. Old favourites like 'Chapel in the Moonlight', 'Sonny Boy' and 'Home on the Range' were trotted out as well as 'We're the Soldiers of the King', but the item that I remember best and which gave me nightmares for weeks was put on by about a dozen of the young men and women. They sat in a group around the 'camp fire' and sang in a very eerie fashion:

A lady stood by the churchyard wall . . .
Oo oo oo oo, oo oo oo oo.
The lady was so gaunt and tall . . .
Oo oo oo oo, oo oo oo oo.
A corpse was being carried in . . .
Oo oo oo oo, oo oo oo oo.
The corpse was pale white and thin . . .
Oo oo oo oo, oo oo oo oo.
Worms crawled in and worms crawled out . . .
Oo oo oo oo, oo oo oo oo.
In through the nose and out of the mouth . . .
Oo oo oo oo, oo oo oo oo.
The lady turned to the corpse and said . . .

Oo oo oo oo, oo oo oo oo.
Will I be like you when I am dead . . .
Oo oo oo oo, oo oo oo oo.
The corpse answered with a groan . . .

And at that the women in the group let out a piercing scream. It frightened the daylights out of me!

As time went by the group put on pretty impressive productions, many of them written by its members. There was a musical about the Tartars with a stirring song:

In the days of Ghengis Khan
Mighty days of Ghengis Khan

The atmosphere that song created as it was sung, off stage, by a group of men, giving an impression of the advancing hordes, was electric. I can feel the excitement still.

There were all sorts of songs written about Camp life, some of them original, some parodies of songs that were popular before we'd been taken prisoner.

Sammy Nissim had brought his trumpet and after he played at a concert he was pressed into service as the camp bugler, sounding the Reveille and lights-out each morning and night. To wake us up he played a few bars of:

Oh it's nice to get up in the morning
But it's nicer to stay in bed . . .

At lights out we got 'Taps':

Day is done,
Gone the sun,
From the Hills,
From the sea,
From the sky,
All is well,
Rest in peace,
God is nigh.

The sporting enthusiasts had brought their cricket, baseball, soccer, rugby and golfing equipment with them, so cricket and baseball teams were selected and a competition got under way. Later a football competition was arranged with Arsenal, Tottenham Hotspurs, Aston Villa and Manchester United as some of the teams. The rivalry was as keen as you'd find anywhere. Teams practised and trained, and strived for supremacy. It was probably our love for and involvement in sport that saw us through the camp. Softball teams with names like the Brooklyn Dodgers and the New York Yankees slugged it out when the parade ground wasn't taken up with cricket, soccer or rugby.

Some of the guards who were keen baseball players used to watch the competition and inevitably a challenge match was arranged between a guards' team and a team from the camp. The Japs treated it as a gala occasion and their team arrived togged out in light grey baseball uniforms, with an insignia embroidered on their shirt fronts, their trousers tucked in their socks and dark grey baseball caps which the catcher and the batsmen wore back to front. They were cheerful and friendly as the game started but after a few innings it was apparent that the guards were quite outclassed by our chaps—some of whom had been professionals before the war. About halfway through the match Tanaka came over to share in his team's victory, but when he saw the score he flew into a rage, shouting and cuffing guards and prisoners alike. The game was disbanded and we were all ordered to our rooms, where we had to remain for the rest of the day.

Next morning at rollcall we were kept waiting for a couple of hours before Tanaka led the guards across to supervise our numbering off. They were a sullen bunch. There was no signs of recognition and gone were the smiles and the camaraderie of the previous day's game. Cuffings and beatings were dealt out without provocation. Bedridden prisoners who until now had always been exempt from parading, were dragged from their rooms and forced to stand and number off with the rest of us. While the sick and the weak fainted, Tanaka gave us another of his interminable lectures on how fortunate we were that the Emperor had seen fit to bring us under his protection. His Divine Personage had shown us a great kindness, and we must be taught gratitude. Life in the camp deteriorated from that day. Shortly afterwards our guards were replaced by a group all but one of whom were sadists.

Two of the new guards were monsters—one named Tanaka (which seemed to be the Nipponese equivalent to Smith) and one we called Pig Face because the description suited him. Hardly a day passed without someone being beaten for some reason real or imagined.

Yamamoto was a little chap even by Japanese standards. He was round and jolly and took every opportunity to show us photos of his wife and children. His shirt was always out at the back, his trousers were usually tied up with a piece of shabby white tape and his sword, which was almost as long as he was, seemed hell-bent on tripping him up when he walked. He was extremely shy and uncontrollably self-conscious if the ladies in the morning rollcalls smiled or winked at him. He'd squirm and try to look away. Then, when the embarrassment was too much for him, he'd run around behind the line only to be confronted with another row of smiling females. Yamamoto gave some light relief to those tedious parades.

Tanaka had been replaced by Hashazumi, who seemed to derive intense pleasure from increasing the suffering of the camp occupants at every opportunity. As soon as he took over, our rations were cut and continued to be reduced at irregular intervals. Whenever Geordie Grant approached Hashazumi about an increase in rations, Hashi got in first by announcing that rations were to be cut still further. We had been getting supplies of soya bean milk for the patients in the hospital. It was white and gluggy like milk that had curdled and I'm sure it was extremely nutritious, but I never acquired a taste for it. Hashi cut out the soya bean milk.

At his first morning rollcall Hashazumi kept us waiting on parade for a couple of hours in the blazing sun before he marched across from the guardhouse with his retinue. A little round man with greying hair and a thick neck, his pig-like eyes peered out at us through small, gold-rimmed glasses with very thick lenses.

In the customary fashion we were called to order,

'Tootskay'

'Attention'

'Bungo'

'Number'

'One, two, three, four . . .'

Hashazumi screamed an order as his face turned crimson. His

neck bulged out over his collar and palpitated like a bullfrog's. He waved his arms and shouted more orders and we wondered, hopefully, if he'd have a seizure. The numbering tapered off and a low murmur went around the parade ground as those who understood Japanese told us that Hashi was outraged that we were not numbering in Japanese. He launched into a screaming lecture, the gist of which was that in camps in England and America, Japanese nationals were expected to number off in English and therefore we would be required to do so in Japanese. He said he would grant us one week in which to learn how to count and from then on all our rollcalls would be conducted only in Japanese.

So were started to practice: 'Ichi, ni, san, shi, go, roko, shchi [or nanna], hatchi, ku, ju, ju ichi, ju ni' and so on.

Some of the older internees found it difficult to remember the sequence until someone came up with: 'Itchy knee sang she. Go loko. See Hashi, could you.' Of course the option of nanna for shchi gave rise to substitutions of 'banana', but on most occasions the Japs let that pass without incident. Some never learnt the system but having mastered one number always stood in the same place in their line.

I found the long parades particularly trying as I'd always had what the kids at school called a 'Japanese' bladder. I could barely last through a class at school without having to 'leave the room'. These long rollcalls were agony. I'd twist and turn and squirm. There was no 'being excused' from parades, so when I could no longer control the urge I'd put my hand in my pocket and squeeze the end of my dick as hard as I could. After an hour or so of this the pain around my kidney region was almost unbearable. When, after an eternity, the rollcall was over, if I hadn't already wet my pants I'd rush to the nearest toilet block to relieve the pressure. The ache in my kidneys was excruciating and for the rest of the day I'd continue to widdle in dribs and drabs every few minutes. Many years later an X-ray revealed a very large extrusion on the side of my bladder which an urologist told me was probably caused by the abnormal pressure to which it had been subjected on those torturous rollcalls.

Sonny Rhees didn't have a father. He was an only child and had been brought up by his mother. He'd been my best friend at school in Shanghai and we'd sat next to each other in the choir stalls at the cathedral on Sunday. Sometimes I'd visit his place to play.

116

He was crossing the parade ground one afternoon when he incurred the wrath of Pig Face. Sonny didn't fare too well during the encounter and, later in hospital developed peritonitis. He died on my eleventh birthday.

My parents had planned a small party for me that afternoon and had invited Sonny and a few other friends of my age. Of course 'party' was somewhat of a misnomer; 'party' infers at least some feasting! We met in the shade of the cyprus grove for the celebration. My brother had somehow acquired a tennis ball which he'd inscribed with my initials in a kind of monogram, and my parents asked Mr Manley, who was expert with paper and mapping pen, to do a sketch of the church for me. We got the news of Sonny's death just before the party was due to start.

· THE · CHURCH ·
· C · A · C ¯ C ´ ·
· YANGCHOW · ~

My eleventh birthday present

Father O'Collins conducted the funeral service in the church up near the guardhouse. Although he'd gone to an Anglican school and sung in an Anglican cathedral choir, Sonny was a Roman Catholic. From my place in the choir stalls I looked down on the small rough-hewn coffin that the camp carpenters had made. Its top was festooned with flowers. A black shawl covering her face, Sonny's mother sat alone in the front pew near the coffin. She'd asked that I sing:

> There's a friend for little children
> Above the bright blue sky . . .

but I'd cried so much I couldn't sing a note.

The service was interrupted by the tramp of boots and the clank of a sword as a Japanese guard came into the church. Father O'Collins stopped the ritual and looked inquiringly towards the disturbance. We were all alarmed and outraged at this intrusion. But it was Yamamoto who stood in the doorway. Slowly he removed his cap, then to our amazement he unbuckled his sword and laid it on the table inside the door. Silently our eyes followed him as with bent head he moved quietly up the aisle, bowed to Sonny's coffin then sat down beside Mrs Rees. We could see his shoulders shaking with the heart rending sobs that racked his body as Father O'Collins resumed the ritual.

After the service the coffin was carried to the small enclosed compound that had been set aside to become the camp cemetery. A lone grave awaited Sonny. A small white cross had been erected at its head and on it were black letters painted in Early English script:

J
H
S

John Rees

R.J.P.

beloved son of Mary Rees

Born 11.7.32
Died 22.6.43

In the months that followed I'd often slip up to the cemetery and sit quietly on my own reading that inscription over and over, then fixing on that final date—22.6.43—a birthday I'd never forget.

Sonny didn't sleep there alone for long. As starvation, disease and maltreatment took their toll over the next couple of years others joined him. Visits to the small graveyard became part of our way of life at Yang Chow.

The Japs used to have 'jousts' which we were obliged to watch. Two Nips would cover themselves with a protective bamboo and canvas armour and a headpiece much like the one fencers wear, then attack each other with bamboo poles in a kind of bayonet duel. We called the contests 'Woosaw' because as the contestant were jockeying for position they'd say, 'Doooor, doooor, doooor . . .' then when making a lunge at their opponent they'd shout, 'Woosaw'.

There was a variation of this sport when instead of prodding at each other with poles, the contestants armed themselves with shorter bamboos like swords, which they used to try to beat each other about the head and shoulders. Although there seemed to be no rules for the contests, there must have been, for at the most unexpected times in the midst of all the shouting, the combatants would stop, bow to each other and leave the ring.

Woosaw affected us in two ways, neither of them pleasant.

The contents of the Red Cross parcels the Japs had commandeered were given out as prizes to the winners in the woosaw contests. We had to stand and watch as our food, cigarettes, razors and medicines were handed out to the Nips.

After woosaw bouts the guards would get into the cheap sake which they drank from large green bottles with white, black and red labels. Then when they were drunk the nastiest of them would come down to take out their aggressions on us. After one drinking session Pig Face was so drunk and so belligerent that he attacked a large ash tree. By the time he'd finished only the handle remained of his sword.

CHAPTER 13

BEDBUGS & MALARIA

A year had passed. It was summer again and the temperatures climbed into the hundreds. On hot days we'd be left to stand, without hats, on the parade ground for hours in the blazing sun. The summer temperatures at Yang Chow were often up around 112° or 113° F (44°C). If we took out our resentment by displaying any insolence towards the guards, they'd retaliate with further beatings and more prolonged rollcalls. The members of the Camp Committee exhorted us to recognise that the Nips had the upper hand and nothing useful could be achieved by antagonising them.

Drawn-out rollcalls weren't the only problems we had to face. As summer moved into full swing so did the bedbugs. They were little grey fellows about the size of fleas that hid during the day in the cracks in our iron bedsteads, or in tiny crevices in the brick walls. But after lights-out they'd swarm in force. You could feel your flesh creep as they crawled all over you hunting for a succulent place to feed, then they'd bite like fury. In the dark you were helpless against them. By morning they'd have swollen to ten times their normal size and when you squashed them a large splotch of black blood would spurt out. They were real brutes and the bites would itch for days. If, in an attempt to get away from their onslaught you were rash enough to get outside your mosquito net or leaned any part of your body against the netting, the mozzies, who'd been droning up near the ceiling awaiting their chance, would swoop and almost carry you away.

The only way to control the bedbugs was to dismantle our beds and take them out into the sunshine where we'd pour boiling water into all the crannies. That posed the dilemma of using up your whole day's hot water ration on bedbug treatment. Most people tried to last two or three weeks without resorting to this drastic measure, especially since that precious water only killed the bugs in the bed frame, not those that hid in the cracks in the walls. We had tried burning out the bugs with candles, but candles were even scarcer than water. Titled people were not spared from the onslaught of the bugs, on summer days Sir Cyril and Lady Young could be seen alongside we common folk, pouring boiling water over their iron bed frames.

Lack of sufficient bathing posed serious hygiene problems. As well as the bedbugs, lice thrived. They lived in our clothing and in our hair, bringing with them the threat of typhus. Then there was scabies and prickly heat, a horrible itchy rash that spread all over the body and from which there was no form of relief. Our skin was red with the combined effect of the rash and constant scratching. On hot, hot days we'd gaze anxiously at the sky hoping for the huge white cumulus clouds that would billow up and bring with them lightning flashes and the crack and rumble of thunder that heralded a storm. If the rain sheeted down we'd strip to our underwear and stand out in the downpour luxuriating in the extravagance of a clean cool shower. There was an acute shortage of soap but the rain brought temporary relief from the combined itching of mosquito, louse and bedbug bites and the burning of prickly heat.

As the months dragged by, the shortage of food was taking its toll. Our systems had been surprisingly resilient but starvation was wearing us down. Even Slop Bucket was looking thin. His clothes hung off him like flapping bags. Without adequate medication, malaria and dysentery were starting to assume epidemic proportions. Our rations had deteriorated to a cup full of rice per person per day and an ounce (about one cubic inch) of pork per person per week, which was barely enough to sustain life much less help build immunity from disease or supply sustenance for a growing lad. The only vegetables we got were turnips which were either as hard as wood or else rotten right through, and chrysanthemum leaves which tasted vile and, when chewed, turned to a hard fibrous mass that was almost impossible to swallow. The stew was like coloured water and often as not tasted of the rancid pork. The flour that was supplied for our bread was the sweepings from the floor of a nearby mill, more dirt than flour and instead of yeast we now got blocks of raw washing soda to make the bread rise. The bread ration had been cut to one slice on alternate days and any bread that wasn't eaten on the day it was baked was a mass of green slime by next morning.

I was constantly famished and at times the hunger pains became almost unbearable. I recall one dinner time I was so ravenous that I devoured my serve of stew in just a few moments. Usually we tried to linger over our meals in the pretence that it made them go further, but on this particular evening my food seemed barely to have touched the sides as it went down, I was crying with hunger, knowing that there would be nothing more until morning. My father, who had just started on his meal, passed his tiffin carrier over to me and insisted that I eat his portion. I was mortified and never again admitted to my parents how hungry I felt. In fact we children started to tease our mother about our rations. Before our days in the Camp if ever we'd turned our noses up at our meal times, Mum would say,

'One day you may be hungry, and then you'll wish you had all this nice food.' We jokingly told her that she'd willed our starvation onto us.

The camp thrived on rumours and there was a new one almost every day: we were all to be released and repatriated to Goa, or Lourenço Marques, or we were to be sent to one of the camps at Pootung, outside Shanghai, or any or all of the above; the war was going well for us; the war was going badly; a new batch of guards was coming; our guards were going to stay for the duration; we'd be getting some more parcels at the end of the month; there wouldn't be any more parcels . . .

Somehow the news reached us that the Canadrome dog-racing track had closed down and all the greyhounds that had been kennelled there had been turned out into the streets. What a field day for Shanghai's butchers. For the next few weeks our pork ration consisted of surprisingly slim rangy 'pigs' but in the stew who could tell the difference? It was food and it tasted better than rotten pork. The kitchen workers used to suffer from what we called 'pork finger'. Any nick from a knife or scratch from a pork bone would quickly become infected, rapidly turning into angry red ulcer-like sores that exuded yellow pus.

The large bamboo water buckets had started to rot so from time to time, under the weight of boiling water a handle would snap splashing scalding water down one side of the carrier. This would make him drop the second bucket, which would scald the other side of his body. The only treatment the doctors had was gentian violet. Some of the young chaps suffered horrific burns which left them terribly scarred.

We children loved the summer days, the endless sunshine, the lingering twilights and the fury of the thunderstorms which blew young birds from their nests. We'd catch and tame them to keep as pets. We fostered doves, rooks, blackbirds and kites, learnt their diets and got up before dawn to catch worms or scrounge a few grains of rice to feed them. Mostly they'd fly off when they got old enough, but some stayed around for the whole of our sojourn in the camp. During the long summer school holidays we spent all our daylight hours out of doors. We played cricket, climbed trees, pitched softballs, and caught and trained crickets for cricket fights. Every morning the Catholic kids had to go to the catechism classes which were conducted under the trees up near the parade ground by Father O'Collins who was an Australian priest from St Columban's Mission at North Essendon. There were also a lot of Jews in the camp and some were very orthodox, in fact one chap had been in training to be a rabbi before being taken prisoner. I remember sitting under the bell tree one evening with one of the Jewish youngsters who had his food bowl on his lap, scanning the sky for the first sign of a star. It was a fast day the Day of Atonement, or the Passover or some such event and in spite of the shortage of rations he was observing the fast which had started the previous evening. Apparently the appearance of a star heralded the coming of dusk and the end of the fast, and so he sat hungrily waiting as we searched for the first faint twinkling star to wink down at us.

Most times the many diversions helped keep our minds off the gnawing pangs of hunger. Our systems had been surprisingly resilient but starvation was wearing us down to the extent that our weakened bodies were no match for the onslaughts of malaria and dysentery which struck again and again.

Inevitably summer passed, giving us relief from the searing heat. As the cooler days started to paint the trees with soft autumn tones, we bade farewell to the cuckoos, finches and orioles as they left for warmer climes. Soon the other birds would follow, leaving behind only the mighty kites to patrol their realm. The north wind held a hint of the chills that were in store when winter closed in again and the snow would start to fall.

Those prisoners who'd thought that the war would be all over in a few weeks and had brought no winter clothes with them were regretting their recklessness. Although many of the POWs had bought codliver oil suits when the store had operated, there was still a grave shortage of warm clothing and bedding. As it grew steadily colder those who had extra shared with those who were without.

On the plus side, the bedbugs modified their onslaught and our sleep was no longer disturbed by them and the drone of swarming mosquitoes. It was a relief to sleep without the restriction of a mosquito net. Although the threat of malaria eased, those of us who had contracted it found that the fever, with its soaring temperatures and violent shivering bouts, recurred every two or three weeks and would continue to do so for many years to come. To everyone's relief the prickly heat tapered off, as did the cramping pains of dysentery, but the cooler weather brought its own share of afflictions. Common colds became all too common and we again kept a safe distance from Slop Bucket. Influenza spread through the camp and the more serious cases developed into pneumonia which could take its victims on a one-way journey to the little graveyard.

The medical situation was extremely grave. It was obvious that many of the sicker prisoners would not survive the winter. The doctors were doing all that they could but without medications and equipment things were getting desperate. Then, by a stroke of luck, Hashazumi's superior officer was stricken with appendicitis. There were no other doctors in Yang Chow, so Hashi ordered that the doctors in our camp carry out the operation, with the threat hanging over them that they'd be executed if the operation was not a success.

The doctors seized on the opportunity to order a huge quantity of medicines and equipment, all of which they insisted were vital to the successful outcome of the impending surgery. Crates and cartons of medical supplies were rushed to the hospital and stored away by willing helpers. Then we waited anxiously. Hashi's boss arrived in the back of a makeshift ambulance which seemed as much in need of surgery as the patient. There was much shouting of orders and cuffing and finally a stretcher bearing a large fat form was manhandled up the steps of the hospital and into the make-shift operating theatre by four perspiring guards. From the groans whenever the stretcher lurched, we gathered that the patient wasn't enjoying the experience. We youngsters exulted in his discomfort.

Now it was Hashazumi's turn to sweat. A mishap in the theatre could mean he, too, would face the execution squad. The minutes passed. Conversation dwindled and we wondered if perhaps something had gone wrong. At last the door opened. Dr Bolton, who taught us physiology in school, removed his mask and proclaimed, much to the relief of us all, that the operation was a success. Hashi became jovial and shook the doctors' hands. In time the patient recovered and the doctors now had a supply of quinine to combat next summer's malaria and all sorts of other supplies to keep the hospital in service.

I was one of the unlucky ones who got malaria badly. It struck suddenly one Friday afternoon when I was at school. At first I felt a bit giddy, my eyes wouldn't focus properly and I felt very cold. Farder Tornton was taking the lesson and noticed that I wasn't well, so sent me home. By the time I got to our room my teeth were chattering and I was shaking uncontrollably. Fortunately Mum was there. She put me into bed and sent for a doctor. My bed was shaking so badly that my brother sat on it to stop it from rattling. By the time the doctor arrived the shivering had stopped, my temperature had climbed to 107° and I was delirious. He rushed me to the hospital where they bathed me with cold water and fanned me with towels to break the fever. Next day my temperature was below normal and, apart from the fact that I was very weak, I felt perfectly well, but the following day the shivering struck once more and my temperature again soared up over 107°. This was the pattern for all the attacks. They'd strike at around two forty-five every second Friday afternoon. At about two o'clock Father Thornton would say in his Irish brogue, 'Begley Two'. (In true British Public School fashion we were called by our surnames followed by a number if there were more than one of us. My brother, who was older, would of course have been Begley One.) 'Oi tink it's toime ya went home, don' choo?'

125

I'd reply that I felt perfectly well, but within a few minutes I'd get the shakes.

Strangely two other internees, Mary Millar, a girl in her late teens and Mr Swanson, a gentleman of middle age, would go down with malaria at the same time. When I came home my mother would call out to Mrs Millar 'How's Mary?' and invariably the answer was 'I've just put her to bed.' The same was true of Mr Swanson. The doctors tried everything they could to help the three of us, but without adequate medication there wasn't much they could do.

'If only we were out of here' they'd say to me, 'we could get you some atabrine. That would fix you up.'

After one particularly bad attack when my temperature reached 108°, the doctors decided to try to poison the malaria by giving the three of us intravenous injections of arsenic. Where the doctors got the arsenic from I don't know, but for several weeks we'd go to the surgery every few days and have these horrible needles in the veins on the inside of our arms. The doctors had to be very careful that the arsenic went into our veins and not into our muscles. The fumes from the injections would well up into our heads and make us quite giddy, but the injections didn't seem to have any effect on the malaria.

An unpleasant side effect that came with every attack of the fever was a bad crop of herpes that covered my right eye. The discharge from the herpes formed scabs that glued my eyelids together. Severe attacks resulted in the herpes forming on the inside of the lid and when these turned to scabs the pain was unbearable. The subsequent scratching caused a corneal ulcer which left a scar that still affects my vision.

However, on the bright side the camp proved pretty good for Billy Spencer. One of the doctors had been a specialist surgeon in Harley Street before coming to China, and he felt confident that he could straighten Billy's legs. He spent a lot of time examining them and finally, with the consent of Billy's parents and the help of other doctors set to work on the straightening process. It took several operations and a lot of exercise on Billy's part, but finally they got him walking almost normally. In fact he was actually able to run in an awkward sort of a fashion and join in some of our games.

CHAPTER 14

THE BELGIANS

The rumour spread through the camp that all Americans were to be repatriated on an exchange basis with Japanese nationals in the USA. At first the rumour was treated with the scepticism accorded to all other rumours, everyone passed it on but nobody really believed it. But then Geordie Grant was called up before Hashazumi who confirmed that the American citizens were to be released. It would be a few weeks before they actually left the camp, but they were to be returned to Shanghai and thence to the States.

Excitement amongst the Americans was beyond belief. They were going home!

It was planned to take the opportunity to try to get information about the camp and our predicament to the Allied forces. When we left Shanghai we had no idea where the Japs were taking us. Most of us had never heard of Yang Chow and we feared that no one knew where we were, so it was vital that as much factual information as possible about us, our whereabouts, physical condition and treatment be documented and sent out with the Americans. We expected that they'd be thoroughly searched before they left the camp, so some ingenious schemes had to be found whereby documents could be concealed without being detected.

With the aid of a magnifying glass and using his skill with mapping pen and Indian ink Mr Manley minutely detailed the information that the Camp Committee wanted sent to the outside world on sheets of Clo Pah. The camp dentist made an upper denture for one of the Americans which had a small watertight compartment with a sliding trapdoor just large enough to hold one sheet of the neatly folded paper. My father stitched several sheets of the notes into the soles of a couple of pairs of shoes. Unless it was raining the owners of the shoes were to wear them as they left the camp.

The great day arrived. The Americans, there were only eight of them, distributed their few surplus belongings amongst those of us who remained and after a thorough search set off through the heavy oak gates to the outside world and freedom. We could only hope that the information they took with them would reach its destination and that, somehow, we too would soon be liberated.

But not yet.

The Japs had a curious habit of breathing loudly and rapidly through open lips and clenched teeth when delivering news that was not pleasant. It made a 'Sheeee ha, Sheeee ha' sort of sound. At rollcall one morning it was announced that about fifty more prisoners were coming into the camp. We were told that it was unfortunate, but due to the shortage of supplies it would not be possible for our rations to be increased to feed these extra people, we'd just have to make the food go further—'So very sorry! Sheeee ha, sheeee ha.'

For crying out loud, we were being starved to death and now the Nips were giving us another fifty mouths to feed!

Later that day the gates opened and in streamed the new inmates carrying their measly belongings. We watched as they were given their lecture on the magnanimity of the wonderful Hirohito and then, as they were dismissed, we milled around to find out something about them. They were Belgians, only a few of whom spoke any English, so communication was a problem. There were no children in the group. The Belgians were allocated the shower house and most of the church for their sleeping quarters. No beds were supplied for them, so they were expected to sleep on straw palliasses on the floor. As some of the Belgians were quite elderly a few of us youngsters gave them our beds.

It was difficult to get to know the Belgians. They seemed distant and reserved, and as language was a significant barrier they kept to themselves. There were often times when they couldn't make themselves understood, so we kids who were learning French at school helped out as interpreters whenever we could.

Shortly after the Belgians' arrival there was a camp concert and one of the items performed was the old song;

128

I'm 'Enery the eighth I am
'Enery the eighth I am, I am.
I got married to the widow next door,
She'd been married seven times before.
Ev'ry one was a 'Enery,
She wouldn't 'ave a Willie or a Sam.
I'm 'er eighth old man called 'Enery.
So 'Enery the eighth I am.

Most of the Belgians were at the concert but had little idea of what was going on until the singer went into his encore:

Je suis Henri le huit je suis.
Henri le huit je suis je suis.
Je marie le veuve d'acôté
Elle se maria sept fois avant
Tout le monde noment Henri
Elle n'etait pas un Guillaum pas un Louis
Je sa huit mari nom Henri
Si Henri le huit je suis.

In spite of the appalling French, the Belgians leapt to their feet, applauding and shouting 'Bravo! Encore, encore!'

The song and the attempt to include the Belgians in the concert crashed the barriers. There was much shaking of hands and slapping of backs and from then on, they became part of the group with the result that their English improved as did our French. We conversed with a mixture of Franglais and sign language to get our meanings across.

As winter set in again, it turned bitterly cold and stayed that way. We made mittens and scarves from any pieces of material that we could scrounge. Few people had more than one thin blanket. The prickly heat was replaced by horrendous chilblains. First our ears were attacked. They became red and itched and burned, then formed scabs which bled and oozed. Then our fingers and toes swelled until the skin split and burst. Like our ears, the splits wept and oozed and the pain was excruciating. We found that we could get temporary relief by rubbing our chilblains with snow. Our ears became very vulnerable to attack from the guards. If we earned their displeasure they took great delight from violently rubbing our ears with their gloved hands. Not only did this stimulate heat in our ears to make them more sensitive, but the rubbing broke the scabs and renewed the bleeding and oozing. The pain was almost unbearable.

Snow fell almost constantly and lay in drifts several feet deep. Temperatures hovered around 12 - 13°F, about 10°C below freezing, the water in the karngs turned to solid ice and icicles hung from the eaves of the buildings. Of course as youngsters we had great fun playing in the snow, making snowmen and having snow fights, but our clothes would get saturated and as we had little chance of drying them out we got terribly cold once our activities ceased. If we were lucky we were allowed to crowd into the kitchen around the huge cauldrons to thaw out, but that was a rare luxury as there was scarcely enough fuel to cook the meals and as those on kitchen duty had to get the meals prepared before the fuel was exhausted they couldn't have us getting under their feet.

On the plus side the snow eased the water shortage. We'd shovel it into the large bamboo buckets to melt it in the kitchen cauldrons for cooking the stew.

However, the morning parades were torturous. Before rollcall was sounded we had to clear trenches in the snow on the parade ground, then we'd stand, interminably in the freezing cold, waiting for the guards. In winter, as punishment, some offenders were made to kneel in the snow for an hour or so. After one of these sessions the victim would be unable to stand and have to be carried indoors and wrapped in blankets to thaw out. Any attempt to warm them quickly would bring on a fresh bout of chilblains.

Our food rations suffered. The scrawny turnips that came in were frostbitten and woody. By the time we'd got our meals the stew was cold and greasy. There were no green vegetables—not even chrysanthemum leaves—and another shortage started to take effect. There wasn't enough fuel to keep the cooking fires and the bakery ovens going. Every spare scrap of wood that could be scrounged was used to feed the cooking fires, but as the shortage became acute we reluctantly had to fell some of the majestic trees in the camp grounds for firewood.

It was unbearably cold in bed at night. The thin blankets we had were no match for the biting frosts. We'd wake in the morning to windows caked with ice and long tapering icicles hanging from eaves and tree branches.

As it got close to Christmas Geordie Grant sought audience with Hashazumi to explain that this was a significant time in the Christian calendar and it would be appreciated if something special could be supplied so we could have a Christmas feast. After much palaver Hashi agreed to let us have some ducks. Shortly before Christmas forty live, brown, very scrawny ducks arrived. We nurtured them with anticipation until the fateful day of the long knives. Forty skinny ducks don't go very far amongst 650 people but it was the thought that counted and we were quite sure that our stew tasted different that Christmas day.

The following week our pork ration did not arrive. When Geordie went to see Hashi he was told that we'd have to do without meat for three months to offset the cost of the ducks!

On Christmas Eve it had snowed heavily. The grounds were covered with a thick white blanket with the limbs of the trees hanging low under their load. However, the snow had stopped by evening when we went carolling around the camp, and, though it was bitterly cold, the sky had cleared to a brilliant moonlit night. 'In the bleak mid winter . . .' had taken on fresh significance for us.

For some time it had become obvious to most of us that the tide of war had started to turn against the Japanese. The first indications came when their treatment of us worsened. Small things that would have passed unnoticed now earned swift, severe and often brutal retribution. Our hopes were confirmed by the newspapers which, although still full of Japanese propaganda, enabled us to plot the course of the war. One month the invincible Japanese forces were defending New Guinea and exacting horrendous punishment on the aggressors. A month or two later when next we saw a newspaper, it would recount how the Japs were attacking the Allied bases on New Guinea and driving them into the sea. And so it went, resounding victories that were easing the Japanese forces ever backward to their home islands. Although we suffered more at the hands of the Nips, we exulted in the news that the Allies were successfully counter-attacking and maybe soon we'd be free.

The Allied advance fuelled more and more rumours—Saipan has fallen; MacArthur's on his way back to the Philippines; they're bombing Okinawa . . .

Meanwhile the camp spies were leaking more and more information to the guards, and although none of it was of any importance it gave the Nips further excuses to mete out punishments. The situation was becoming intolerable, especially with regard to one of the spies who flaunted his privileged position, ridiculed the Allied forces and boasted of how well he'd be looked after by the Japs when they'd won the war.

CHAPTER 15

IS IT OVER?

The summer of '45 was particularly hot and the rollcalls seemed interminable. There was a grave shortage of water and we were all weak from the effects of prolonged malnutrition. More and more of us went down with beri-beri and dysentery, but we still met with Mr Quincy at daybreak every morning for our physical work-out and we still participated in sports at every opportunity.

We were spurred on by an overall feeling of optimism. The war news, fed by countless rumours, was good and getting better. We were sure that liberation day must be getting close, when one clear sunny day we thought we heard a faint drone, a distant hum like the sound of bees swarming. We listened and it was gone, then we heard it again. It came and went in waves. Could it be the sound of aircraft? That would be too much to hope for. Now it was more distinct and as we scanned the sky, from the east we saw way, way up, the glint of the sun against something silver. Yes, up towards the sound we could see tiny shining shapes in the sky. These planes were the first signs of war activity we had seen since we'd been in the camp. The planes drifted over and were gone. Maybe that the Nips were on the run. As we were revelling in this conjecture we heard the rumble of distant thunder. Bombs? Not bombs! They couldn't have been Allied planes, that wouldn't be possible! But wasn't that bombing we'd heard? The rumours flew around the camp, then after a few days the planes returned. This time we were sure it was a high-level bombing raid. The rumble of explosions was more distinct. The raids became more and more frequent.

Swearing us to secrecy, the moordung amahs told us that the Japanese were retreating on all fronts and the raids had been on an ammunition dump near Chin Kiang. But the word got to the Japs through one of the spies. A special rollcall was ordered and we were

marched to the area outside Hashazumi's house where we were
formed into a large circle. After a few minutes Pig Face, Tanaka and
a couple of the other guards came into the ring followed by a group
of Chinese women who we recognised to be our mordung amahs.
They wore traditional black calico jackets and trousers and were
being led by ropes fastened around their throats. Hashi followed
close behind and gave another of his lectures.

'What's he saying?'

'Shsh I can't hear . . . I think its something about obedience to
authority and the greatness of Hirohito.'

After the speech more guards entered the ring carrying bamboo
poles about five feet long and an inch and a half in diameter. The
poles had been split down their length leaving a handle section about
eighteen inches long. The splits left slivers of bamboo about a quarter
of an inch wide. The guards went across to where the amahs were
tethered and stripped them naked, then set about beating them with
the split bamboo poles. Whenever the poles struck the splits would
open, then spring closed again, pinching the skin. As the poles were
pulled back for the next blow the flesh was ripped from the women's
bodies. Their screams were pitiful but the Japs were without mercy.
Several of the POWs tried to break ranks to intervene but they were
clubbed with rifle butts. Only when the women were shapeless blobs
of bleeding flesh on the ground did the torture stop. Then we were
marched back to the parade ground and dismissed.

Another rumour slipped around the camp, this one whispered
secretly between groups when they met out in the grounds. No one
dared speak of it indoors. I heard it through Joey Azachee, who
knew everything that went on in the camp. One of the many
anomalies about the camp was that although the Japs were fanatical
about us all being in our rooms for the night rollcall, no check seemed
to be made on what happened after lights-out.

On the next moonless night I waited until everyone in the room
was asleep then sneaked silently from my bed and crept noiselessly
out into the yard, pulling my clothes over my pyjamas. It was pitch
dark and overcast. I ran across to the bell tree and stood, holding my
breath, waiting. The camp was still. There was no one else about so
I sprinted across to the grove of cypruses and pressed my body against
a tree trunk while I caught my breath.

'Shut up Pop. Ya makin' more noise than a herd o' elephants. Wot ya tryin' to do, wake the whole damn camp?'

It was Joey. The kids called me 'Pop' because I had a particularly distended 'pop' belly. 'They're over there under that elm so don' move or talk or nothin', OK?'

I peered through the blackness but couldn't make out anything but the trunk of the elm tree. We waited.

'He's coming' Joey whispered as, silhouetted against the skyline between where we stood and the guardhouse we could see a shadow moving towards us. The shadow got close to the elm tree before the trunk materialised into three figures. I heard a scuffle, dull thuds a grunting sound and the figures melted into the night.

'Hell we betta get outa here,' Joey whispered urgently, 'an' if you tell anybody about this Pop, I'll cut ya.' And he was gone. I had no doubt he would have.

I stood holding my breath, straining my ears, there was only silence so I dashed for the bell tree, regained my breath and sneaked back to our room, stripping off my outer clothes as I went. The men were snoring and the room was filled with snuffling sleep noises. Back in the security of my bed I lay barely daring to breathe.

I must have slept because I awoke to a commotion. Voices were shouting, feet were running, the camp bell was tolling.

It seems that sometime during the night, the best known camp spy had been badly beaten up under the large elm tree. Nobody knew how it happened or why he would have been out of his room after lights out. The Japs held lengthy interrogations but all the POWs insisted they knew nothing. He had been in his room at rollcall and lights-out and as everyone was confined to their rooms until morning, we had to consider that he had fallen foul of some Chinese intruders who must have climbed the wall into the camp. That was the only story the Nips were able to get from anyone in the camp and as neither Joey nor I had been there when it happened, we couldn't have told otherwise even if we'd been asked.

We'd become quite friendly with Yamamoto. Under different circumstances in a different place at a different time Yamamoto would have been a pleasant, jolly chap. He never took part in any of the acts of brutality that seemed to be such fun for many of the other guards, and since Sonny's funeral had done his best to make life a little less horrendous for us children whenever he could. He was a little round fellow with a shaved head and sometimes in the evenings he'd sit and chat with us on the bench under the bell tree. His English was as hopeless as was our Japanese, but we managed some sort of communication. It was now no secret that things were going very badly for Japan and as Japanese tradition demanded that its soldiers could not surrender, Yamamoto knew that he'd have to commit harakiri. I remembered the time on the train and tried to imagine little Yamamoto kneeling on his mat plunging a large knife deep into his pudgy stomach. The tears in his eyes didn't go unnoticed as he showed us photos of the wife and family he knew he would never see again.

Our treatment seemed to be getting better. Although our rations had deteriorated to the point where there was hardly enough stew to go around, the guards seemed anxious to ingratiate themselves with the prisoners wherever possible. Rollcalls became more informal with banter going unchecked and, at times, even mirth among the Japs. Our optimism grew by the day as it became apparent that the guards spent less time patrolling the camp grounds. We were sure that the war would soon be over and talked at length of our victory celebrations. We fantasised over the sumptuous feasts we'd have when at last we were back in Shanghai again. Old sheets and other scraps of cloth were cut and hemmed to make large flags. Coloured paint was somehow scrounged to turn them into a Union Jack and a Belgian flag. As Australians we made an Australian flag with its Union Jack over a seven-pointed star and the Southern Cross. The flags were hidden away in the PWD section awaiting the great day when we would be able to hoist them and proclaim our freedom.

But we were still starved of real news. There was the usual run of rumours but the newspapers had stopped, and after the incident with the mordung amahs there was a decided reluctance on the part of any Chinese to give us word of the outside world.

One afternoon we saw a Chinese soldier walking along the city wall which overlooked the camp. He called out, asking what we were doing in there, and when we replied that we were prisoners of the Japs, he said, 'But the war's been over for three weeks. You should be free.'

In response to our disbelief, he rolled a newspaper in a rock and threw it over the wall to us.

My father was one of the few people in the camp who could read Chinese and he confirmed what the soldier was saying. By now a crowd of us had gathered near the wall, and after much more calling back and forth and more details of Japan's capitulation, Geordie Grant and my dad went up to see Hashazumi.

Hashi told them he'd heard nothing,

'Well if the war's over,' Geordie said. 'We aren't going to parade for you every day.' 'Please yourselves,' Hashazumi replied.

So that was it. Apparently the war was over—well, we hoped it was, but we were still in the camp. We knew that we were in Yang Chow, but we weren't too sure precisely how we would get back to Shanghai. We had no idea what the Chinese attitude towards us would be and, in spite of Geordie's stand with Hashi, we were still surrounded by armed guards. So it was decided that we'd better stay put.

CHAPTER 16

HEAVENSENT

At a specially convened meeting of the Camp Committee it was decided that for the time being we should remain in the camp, where at least we had some food. Attempts would be made to contact the Chinese and through them get word to the outside world of our predicament. But contact with the Chinese proved to be difficult. The Japs were still armed and any Chinese who came into the camp were very nervous about what they said or did. It was suggested that a couple of the fitter young men could set off in the hope of finding their way to Shanghai. There was no shortage of volunteers, but with neither money nor food the Committee ruled this out as impractical.

As we pondered the problem, the solution walked in through the main gates in the form of a small contingent of American soldiers under the command of a Captain Cox. They looked so smart in their beautifully pressed khaki uniforms with their neat forage caps set at a rakish angle and their highly polished shoes. Delirious with delight, we mobbed them and cheered. This was really Victory day! The flags came out of hiding, bamboo poles were found from somewhere and our flags proudly unfurled to the breeze.

But our excitement was short-lived. Captain Cox cautioned that we must not offend the Japanese and the flags had to come down. We had no idea how the Japanese would react, he told us, and to our astonishment the Americans surrendered their weapons to the Nips and became prisoners with us!

That night we crammed into the dining hall to hear a lecture from Captain Cox about the war and America's victory. He told of the marvellous American inventions that had expedited that victory. This thing, that he called 'RAGAR', had enabled the Allied forces to actually 'see' things that were many miles away over the horizon, making it possible for our troops to bombard ships that would otherwise have been out of sight, or shoot down planes before they came into view. He went on to tell of the super bomb that the Americans had dropped on a place called Hiroshima—he pronounced it 'Herosheema'. It was an 'atomic' bomb which was of unbelievable force, many, many times more powerful than the blockbusters of the German blitz, but it was only the size of a tennis ball, he said, and had to be dropped by parachute so it would explode a hundred feet above ground level. Although the blast from these bombs spread out in a cone from the detonation point and levelled everything that was above ground, he told us that it had no effect on anything that was below ground level. He gave us the example of a soldier who had jumped into a dug-out just as the bomb had exploded. Although his body was below ground level, his right elbow, which had been above ground and in the path of the blast, was blown off. Apart from this the soldier was not injured.

After the bomb was dropped on Hiroshima, he said, the Japanese were called upon to surrender. When they hadn't done so after several days a second bomb was dropped. This one on Nagasaki. After the second bomb the Japs capitulated.

We were led to understand that the after-effects of these bombs were such that it would be impossible for any crops to be grown in the area or any human habitation to take place. Hiroshima and Nagasaki would be deserts for at least a hundred years.

The Americans brought with them a supply of razor blades, candy bars, Chesterfield and Camel cigarettes—the only cigarette with the factory on the packet, someone quipped—and some of the prettier girls even managed to score some nylon stockings. We kids heard all sorts of rumours as to how they'd got them but we never saw any of the Americans walking the way Joey had demonstrated to us in our hideout.

A few days after the arrival of the Yanks the gate again opened to admit a visitor. This time it was a British officer named Captain Martin. He wore a red beret, sported a rather thick moustache and was accompanied by two sick-bay attendants.

'What the bloody hell's going on here?' he roared and stormed over to the guardhouse where he disarmed the guards, gave the

Americans back their weapons, flung open the gates and ordered that we raise our flags immediately and leave them up. At last the war was over for us, really over.

Captain Martin led a search of Hashi's residence, seizing his files. In them were found detailed plans for our extermination. Plan 1 was that we were to be herded to an extermination camp, preferably a cave, where we would be sealed in and left to die of starvation. This plan, we later learnt, had already been put into effect at some camps! If there was insufficient time to implement plan 1, then Hashazumi was to adopt plan 2 wherein we were to be stood up against the back wall of the camp and machine-gunned. Plan 2 was to be adopted only as a last resort because it would use up valuable ammunition. For us at least, 'the bomb' was not dropped in vain nor was it dropped a day too soon.

At a camp concert that night we were introduced to a new song:

We're going home, we're going home,
We're on the way that leads to home,
We've had enough of living rough,
And now we want the real stuff
In home sweet, home.
No more eating of Yang Chow stew,
No more sharing a room with you,
For there's no place like home,
There's no place like home . . .

Well, we were free but not yet freed. We were still stuck in Yang Chow and Captain Martin recommended that we stay in the compound while a selected few went out to test the feelings of the Chinese. Our rations, meagre as they were, were still coming in but we had no money to purchase more. Captain Cox had a small radio. Under Captain Martin's instructions he contacted Shanghai to arrange for food to be sent to us.

A couple of days later a message came through that we were to make two large PW signs. One was to be placed on the roof of house 3A and the other in the middle of the parade ground. A couple of threadbare sheets were torn up to make the signs and next day three four-engined B29 Super Fortresses buzzed the camp, then, as we waved and cheered, circled up to about 5 000 feet where they did a couple more passes over the camp. As we watched fascinated, their bomb bays opened and tiny black dots fell towards us. As the dots came closer, some changed colour and started to drift, but the others kept coming, getting bigger and bigger, tumbling end over end. They were 44-gallon drums, some single, some welded together, which contained pork and beans and clingstone peaches or spaghetti. Others had powdered milk, chocolates, cheese, coffee and biscuits. The coloured ones were attached to parachutes which opened and took them drifting off into the distance where no doubt some lucky Chinese put them to good use. The black ones were drums that had ripped away from their chutes and rained on us like bombs. Exploding on impact they spewed peaches, spaghetti and pork and beans in all directions. A couple were sitting in their room on the third floor of house 3A watching the planes through their window. A double 44 gallon missile made a direct hit through the loop of the P just above their heads. Bursting on impact it ripped straight through the roof, landing on a bed a couple of feet from where they were seated, proceeded on down, taking the bed with it to the second floor where it gave a repeat performance and so on to the ground floor spraying a mixture of pork and beans and peaches in its wake.

After so long without, the sight of so much food was overwhelming. Some of the POWs wallowed in it, shovelling the mixture into their mouths, only to be violently ill as their digestive systems rebelled against the unaccustomed richness. Many fled desperately searching for places to hide, terrified by the fury of the bombardment. The Camp Committee pleaded with Captain Cox to stop the waste.

'There's plenty more where that came from.' was his reply.

Eventually the barrage ceased. The huge bombers flew in low over the camp, waggled their wings in a gesture of farewell, and disappeared into the distance.

The food and other supplies were gathered and distributed by the Camp Committee. Feasts were held all over the camp. At long last food, food and still more food! My parents rationed us to a 'victory feast' of two small cracker biscuits each with butter and cheese, and a cup of instant coffee with powdered milk and sugar, but our systems couldn't cope with the sudden plenty. Mum suffered a severe bilious attack. Many of the internees who had been less prudent were violently ill. Some died.

A week after the first food drop, the planes came over again. Either they were better prepared or we were not taken so much by surprise, but the bombardment seemed to be less terrifying and a lot more successful. Many more of the multi-coloured parachutes opened and we were able to retrieve most of the supplies. Now we had plenty of food, good wholesome food. As our systems adapted we were able to eat more and some flesh started to grow over our bones. We were still desperate to get away from Yang Chow and back to Shanghai but the problem of transport had yet to be overcome.

Unexpectedly, Geoff Manley became despondent and lay on his bed saying he'd never get out of the camp alive. He had always appeared to be in good health, was in his early twenties and involved in many camp activities. Attempts to break his depression were to no avail and within a week he was dead. Several other POWs were in the same way. The doctors could find no explanation. These chaps were overcome by melancholy and dropped their bundle. No amount of jollying-up could break them from their lethargy.

During this waiting time we received a surprising visit from an old Chinese friend, Chow Shen Shung (Mr Chow), who arrived at the camp with gifts for the family. My parents had known him years earlier in Shanghai, but how he located us and got all the way to Yang Chow I don't know. He brought with him a live white leghorn hen, several pieces of lacquerwork and a Chinese silver dollar which he gave me—I have it still. The chicken I kept as a pet until we left the camp. She wasn't a prolific layer but we didn't have the heart to eat her. After all we no longer needed the food. The lacquerwork stayed in the family for many years.

A few days later a RAF Dakota flew low over the camp, its side doors open with a couple of crew men waving to us as the plane made some passes over the camp. By radio they told us that they carried more supplies for us and on the next pass a large crate was pushed out the side door. A blue parachute opened and the crate landed gently in the middle of the parade ground. The plane dropped ten crates, landing all of them in almost the same spot. The crates contained food, much-needed medication and a more powerful radio for us to keep in contact with the outside world.

At last word came through that we were to be returned to Shanghai. The very sick were taken out first then the rest of us left in groups in much the same order as we'd arrived. Gathering our few belongings—all that we had left in the world—we set off cheering and singing to board a boat for the trip back down the Grand Canal to Chin Kiang. The two and half years since we'd arrived seemed lifetimes ago. So much had changed! Inflation caused by the distribution of Japanese occupation money had rendered the Chinese currency valueless. When we'd gone into the Camp in 1943, the Chinese dollar had been divided into 100 cents and each cent was further divided into four coppers and those coppers had some buying power. Now sitting opposite us on the barge was a Chinese peasant woman who was eating a pear. When she'd finished she threw the core out the window, reached into her bag, took out a $500 bill, wiped her fingers on it and then threw *it* out the window! I remember little else of the trip other than that we were met at Chin Kiang by an RN troop-carrier which took us on to Shanghai where representatives from the Red Cross took us in charge, gave us thorough medical examinations and set us up in temporary accommodation in tenement buildings where we were crowded in with many other recently released internees.

Shanghai was a bare shell of its former self. Few services remained and those that did spent much time broken down. Public transport was almost nonexistent. Businessmen found that their enterprises were gone, their homes had been ransacked, any fittings of value had been stolen, their personal possessions had been looted and their life's work was in ruins. Some couldn't face the prospect of starting all over again and committed suicide. I remember a group of us were standing outside Broadway Mansions one afternoon when one of the men from our camp jumped to his death. We heard someone scream. Looking up we saw him looping through the air towards us. He hit the ground with a dull thud, bounced once and lay still.

We had no money and yet again the Red Cross came to our aid. CRB, the Japanese Occupation Money, was being eroded daily, almost hourly, by galloping inflation. When you went shopping you took a large suitcase with you to carry the money, but you could bring your purchases home in a small bag. An egg cost $3 000. My mother bought me a pair of poor quality sandshoes for $250 000.

The smallest negotiable note was a $500 bill. If and when the trams were running, a single-section fare was $1 000. Money-changers sat at every corner and the exchange rates changed constantly. If you didn't spend your money quickly it would devalue alarmingly in a few hours. On payday shop workers came home in rickshaws with their salaries packed in bundles of banknotes all around them.

To compensate for the lack of public transport the drivers of all occupation force vehicles were instructed to offer us lifts whenever possible, so a more or less regular truck service was available to carry us around the city. We spent much of our time trying to locate old friends who'd been sent to different camps and enjoyed some happy reunions. Too often, as in the case of Eric Liddell, our friends had not made it through to the end of the war. We'd never again hear him relate the story of his Olympic victory.

There was a grave shortage of gasoline in Shanghai so most of the privately owned cars and trucks had gas producers mounted on their running boards, small furnaces that converted coal into a gas that could be burnt in the engines' combustion system. The gas produced was not very efficient and resulted in a large loss of power, it also had a rather disastrous effect on cylinder heads and combustion chambers, but at least it meant that the vehicles were kept mobile.

My father was anxious to get back to Hong Kong to re-establish the work he'd been doing when he was taken prisoner, and by pulling a few strings was able to hitch a ride there on an RAF Catalina flying boat. We went down to the Bund to see him off. The 'Cat' was an awkward looking thing wallowing there in the muddy water with its high tail fin and engines set up on top of the wings. It looked as if it couldn't possibly fly. Dad was ferried over to it in an air force motor launch. Soon afterwards, we heard the Cat's engines roar into life as its spinning propellers churned the river into a foam. The plane moved forward slowly and as it gathered speed its hull eased out of the water. For a short time the plane skimmed the surface seeming reluctant to leave the river, then it climbed lazily upwards, circled the city several times, waggled its wings in salute and headed south.

Meanwhile Mum was desperately trying to arrange for our repatriation to Australia and succeeded in getting places on a Royal

Navy troop transport bound for Hong Kong. Two corvettes escorted us on the long slow voyage, combing the sea on the lookout for unexploded mines. Whenever a mine was sighted our ship would be warned to proceed with caution while our escorts detonated the mine with gunfire. It was great sport to watch the huge water spouts as the mines exploded. A couple of times the mines were too close before they were spotted, so we'd reduce speed to a crawl and watch nervously as the mine with its menacing, protruding spikes bobbed slowly past us until it was far enough astern for one of the escorts to blow it up.

We slept in hammocks slung below decks and ate our meals off large trestle tables in the mess deck. We were scheduled to help with food preparation and my daily tasks mainly comprised hours labouring over a large tub of water, peeling potatoes. On the way down the coast we ran into a heavy storm and because of the difficulty keeping an adequate mine watch, the convoy considered returning to Shanghai. But the ship rode it out and steamed into Hong Kong with little more to report than numerous cases of seasickness.

CHAPTER 17

THE VICTORIOUS

Hong Kong had seen more of the war than Shanghai. The island had been heavily bombed and the mainland showed the marks of the retaliatory bombardment. We moved into a flat at Kowloon not far from Kai Tak airport. There was a large contingent of RAF personnel living there under canvas so we had a very good transport service almost at our doorstep.

Although it was a relief to get to Hong Kong, where life seemed much less hectic than it had been in Shanghai, we were still a long way from Australia. The shortage of food was still a major problem but our diet was augmented by military K-Rations and generous handouts from the troops. At least here the inflation was under control.

My brother and I ranged all over Kowloon and spent a lot of our time at the YMCA where we had use of the gymnasium and the swimming pool. Nude bathing was still the rule so our lack of bathing costumes posed no problem. We also attended the variety shows that were staged at the YM to entertain the troops. Amongst the entertainers were stand-up comedians who told jokes that had the servicemen in fits. In spite of my grounding in the facts of life by Joey Azachee, most of these jokes went over my head, but I'd laugh anyhow. There were also singers, magicians and a ventriloquist with a very precocious doll and a pretty assistant who wore what was considered in those days to be a very daring two-piece bathing suit which brought cheers of approval from the troops. They'd shriek with delight at the liberties the doll took with this beautiful young lady who seemed oblivious of its existence. At every session there'd be a sing-along with the words of the songs projected onto a screen and a bouncing ball moving along to let us know when the words were to be sung. I learnt new songs that had become popular during the war: 'Don't Fence Me In', 'What Do You Know She Smiled at Me in my Dreams Last Night', 'The Echo Told Me a Lie', 'I'll be Home for Christmas', 'I'm Riding for a Fall', 'Lilli Marlene', 'A Nightingale Sang in Barclay Square' and many others. 'There'll Always Be an England' usually got an airing and of course 'Open the Door Richard'—We were told that the song on the flip side of the record was 'Don't Close it on Me Dick'!

Every morning a group of Japanese prisoners was herded up the streets at a brisk jogtrot by a team of Allied soldiers driving Jeeps. These prisoners were detailed to carry out the housework for all the ex-POWs who were in Hong Kong at the time. A couple of our soldiers would sit on the bonnets of the Jeeps wielding large sticks which they'd use to make sure the Nips didn't break ranks or lag behind.

Each morning two of the prisoners were dropped off at our flat, where they were required to bow respectfully to my mother and then do our chores. They'd be picked up again in the afternoon for the jog back to their camp. In spite of our past treatment, my mother felt sorry for these prisoners, although she was under strict instructions that they were to be given neither food nor drink and no attempt should be made to befriend them in case this was interpreted as weakness and they took advantage of her. I must confess I thought this was reasonable enough, considering that the Japs deserved everything that was coming to them, but I noticed that on a hot day the prisoners somehow got a cool drink and there was always something left over from a our tiffin which found its way to them. But then Mum always had been a bit of a softie, so we said nothing about it.

The Japs wore their greenish khaki uniforms and little caps, now stripped of any badges of rank, and their ankle-length black rubberised canvas boots which separated the big toe from the rest of the foot. They were put to work all over Hong Kong to restore some of the infrastructure that had be wiped out by the war. There were a couple of unfortunate incidents of reprisals against them but these appeared to be rather isolated, though with no newspapers and little local news we hadn't much knowledge of what actually went on in Hong Kong other than the rumours, of which there were plenty.

We were befriended by a number of servicemen who, perhaps out of pity for our condition, or maybe because they missed their own families, used to give us all sorts of goodies. One chap who was particularly kind to me was LAC William Sorefleet. Will treated me like a kid brother and when he was off-duty took me tripping all over Kowloon. Sometimes we'd hitch a ride on a landing barge or large amphibious DUKW across to the island for a trip up the peak. Bill gave me a forage cap with an RAF badge and rounds of .303 rifle bullets and some .5 Spitfire cannon shells. He showed me how to remove the head from a bullet and lay out the thin spaghetti-like sticks of cordite to form the letters of my name, then light one end and burn my name into the concrete of the footpath. Some bullets only had black powdered cordite in them, which wasn't much use for anything. You could light it but it just went up with a poof. He gave me carvings he'd made from pieces of perspex and a couple of watches he'd taken from Jap prisoners which had English names engraved on their backs.

Will invited me to his camp at Kai Tak, promising to show me over the Spitfires and some of the other planes that he looked after. So one afternoon I walked out to the airport. Before me was an ocean of military tents. As I'd not thought to ask Will where he was camped, I wandered over to one of the tents and asked if anyone knew where I could find LAC William Sorefleet. There were about a dozen airmen in the tent and one of them said,

'William Sorefleet? Come in, sonny, come on in. No I don't know William Sorefleet, do you Frank?'

'William Sorefleet? No not me, what about you, Jack?'

'Never heard of him.' replied Jack.

I didn't know why, but I was starting to feel uneasy. All the servicemen that I'd met in the past had been friendly and jovial, but these chaps were different somehow. They weren't offensive but something seemed amiss, so I edged towards the entry flap but found my exit blocked by a couple of them. They took me by the arms and led me back into the middle of the tent saying, 'Don't be in a hurry sonny, you want to find your Willie don't you? Well we're going to help you.'

I started to panic. 'Let me go.' I called out. 'I want to go. Please let me go.'

They were laughing and the two who were holding me twisted my arms behind my back while some of the others pulled down my shorts. One of them grabbed my penis and gave it a tug, shouting, 'I've found his Willie, here it is!'

I was terrified. I struggled and tried to call out, but they forced me face down onto one of the camp stretchers and pushed a gag into my mouth. Then, tying some ropes around my ankles they spread my legs apart. While a couple of them held me they each took it in turns to rape me. The pain as they entered me increased my terror. Vainly I tried to kick, I tried to scream, I was sobbing with fright and outrage.

At last it was over. The cords were removed from my legs, the gag was taken out of my mouth, they released my arms and I struggled to pull on my pants. One of them opened the tent flap and I bolted for freedom. Sobbing, I ran all the way home not daring to look back in case they were after me. When I got back to the flat I sneaked up to my bedroom without being seen, and after I'd rinsed the blood from my underpants, I hid until my terror had subsided. Fortunately my socks covered the rope marks on my ankles. I never breathed a word to anyone about my experience. If my father found out I was sure that I'd be in terrible trouble.

CHAPTER 18

HOMECOMING

In spite of my parents' desperate attempts to get us repatriated—it seemed that everyone in Hong Kong wanted to leave the place—it was impossible to get a berth on a ship and, worse still, none of the ships was heading for Australia. They were all bound for the UK. My father had tried unsuccessfully to contact Mr Drakeford, the Minister for Air for the Australian government in the hope of getting us out on a RAAF flight. But Hong Kong proved to be no different from any other place in the world. It's not what you know, but who you know that counts!

A young lady my parents had known in Shanghai was now in Hong Kong and 'keeping company' with a wing commander in the RAAF. They came around to our place for tiffin one Sunday and when my parents expressed their frustration at not being able get out of Hong Kong the wing commander assured us that he would sort it out for us. Within the week we had received a message to say that we were to fly out to Australia on an RAAF DC3 Dakota troop transport that was leaving the following week. Just like that, no red tape, no hassles, nothing! After weeks of lobbying pleading, phoning and cajoling, a casual remark over lunch and everything was arranged.

We were at Kai Tak just before four in the morning, rugged up against the cold. In the early morning darkness we could see the Dakota silhouetted against the skyline. It looked enormous with its nose pointed skywards. Further to the left was the black bulk of the mountain that skirts Kai Tak airport. There were two or three groups, about a dozen people in all, and it seemed that we were all going out on the same flight. We stood on the tarmac whispering to each other, overcome by feelings of awe and fear. Dad was the only member of our family who'd flown before and as he had decided to remain in

Hong Kong for another six months to re-establish the work he'd been doing prior to the war, we were to undertake this terrifying experience without him.

Shortly an RAAF officer came over to tell us that it was time to go. We said our farewells and the officer ushered us towards the aircraft. Its side door was open and we clambered aboard up a small set of aluminium steps that hooked on just below the doorway. The interior of the aircraft, which was not lined, sloped downwards towards the tail so it was awkward trying to move around inside. We strapped ourselves onto bench-type seats that ran along both sides of the plane and faced each other across the bags of mail and other freight that was lashed in the centre of the plane, covered with a large net to hold it in place. The seats, which were made of aluminium framing covered with khaki webbing, were very uncomfortable and had been designed to fold up against the fuselage to make room for more cargo. The plane's windows were made of clear perspex, with a round hole about two inches in diameter in the middle that was closed with a black rubber stopper, like a bath plug, which could be removed to provide ventilation. There was a small door at the rear and one at the front that closed off the cockpit area.

After we were all settled the cockpit door opened and ducking through the small opening, the pilot and co-pilot came into the main cabin to introduce themselves and check to see that the side door was properly closed and that we were properly strapped in. They told us that there was a toilet behind the rear door and that we had been cleared for take off in fifteen minutes at 5 a.m. It was still pitch dark outside. They chatted for a few more minutes, doing their best to allay our nervousness, then returned to their domain at the front.

A few minutes later there was a whirring sound and the port-side propeller started to turn slowly. It turned for several seconds before the engine coughed, caught, coughed again and then backfired, shooting out a huge tongue of orange/red flame. That was enough for me, I undid my seatbelt and bolted for the door. My brother grabbed me, wrestled me back to my seat, sat me down and refastened my belt. The propeller swung a few more times and soon the engine came to life with a deafening roar. The roar increased in volume then eased off a little as the starboard propeller started to turn. Then the whole plane shook as the engine speeds increased. After a few minutes the roar settled to a constant sound and the plane moved slowly forward. We taxied to the end of the runway and stopped while the pilots did their pre-flight checks. The rudder, elevators and flaps were tested, the port engine was revved up and brought back to idle, then the starboard engine went through the same drill. When both engines were accelerated to full throttle and the whole plane seemed to be shaking uncontrollably, the brakes were released and we lumbered slowly down the runway, gathering speed until the plane levelled up as the tail wheel lifted off the ground. A little further down the runway we felt the whole plane lift, then bank gently as it turned in a large circle slowly spiralling up and up clear of the mountains and the lights of Hong Kong far below. As we climbed higher dawn broke and the rays of sunshine sliced through the clouds on the eastern horizon. It was Tuesday, 3 December 1945, and we were on our way home.

We flew until late afternoon and that first day was fairly uneventful. Once the plane was at its cruising altitude of around 6 000 feet the engines' roar reduced as the props were feathered. Then to our consternation the crew came back to join us in the main cabin for a chat and a smoke.

'But who's flying plane?' Mum asked in horror.

'Ar, George has got it under control.' said the pilot,

We hadn't seen anyone called George, in fact we were sure that there were only the two airman up front.

'Who's George?'

It seems that George was the automatic pilot and once we were on course the human pilot switched control over to George who monitored altitude, speed and direction keeping us flying more or less where we were headed. In time we got used to George. The crew told us that we could undo our seatbelts and move around the cabin if necessary, but to maintain the balance and trim of the aircraft they asked us to restrict our movements as much as possible. They had military rations for us to eat and some thermoses of hot coffee.

The plane's fuselage tapered towards the rear, which meant that the area occupied by the toilet was rather confined. Inside the small cubicle was a pedestal over a hole that went out into space. Anything that was deposited there went straight into the open air. It was reminiscent of the joke we kids used to tell of the minister who was saying his grace before preparing a meal. As a plane flew overhead, he stood with frying pan in hand and eyes closed praying, 'All good gifts around us are sent from Heaven above.' Then opening his eyes he found sausages!

It was a long boring flight. We sat, we talked, we read, we took turns sleeping on the bags of mail until late in the afternoon when the pilot told us we were about to start our descent to Leyte in the Philippines. The island slowly came up to meet us and we could make out the wind sock and the runway. We could see coconut palms and jungle green tents stretching off in all directions. Soon the ground was rushing towards us and there was a grinding sound as our wheels touched in a three-point landing The plane lifted a bit, then settled and reduced speed rapidly as we taxied to a group of tents where a Red Cross vehicle was parked.

The engines were cut and the large propellers slowed to a stop. The side door opened the steps were hooked into place and we clambered down to the ground. It was hot. Hot and steamy. As we were ushered into the Red Cross tent, the thing that stuck me most was how yellow everyone was. All the soldiers had bright yellow skins and their eyeballs were yellow instead of white. They'd been taking atabrine as an anti-malarial prophylactic and it stained their skin, their eyeballs, their perspiration and their urine. I'd been put on atabrine as soon as we got to Shanghai and, although it had eased the crippling bouts of malaria, it hadn't yet turned me bright yellow.

We were served a hearty meal in the Red Cross tent and then driven across to the tents where we were to spend the night. My brother and I were in a tent with some US Marines. There seemed to be a constant stream of American servicemen visiting our tent, bringing us candy, chocolate bars and chewing gum. They kept asking me how I was feeling and when they thought I wasn't listening I'd hear them say 'Have you ever seen anything like that starved kid?' or 'Poor little guy. D'ya think he'll make it?'

That night there was a movie show. We sat on the ground between the projector and a large sheet spread between two coconut palms. The film was *Wuthering Heights* and that horseman with the black cape riding across the moors gave me nightmares. It started to pelt down rain just as the show ended. A big soldier picked me up bodily and ran with me back to our tent where, although we were tired and had been warned that we'd be called at 4.30a.m. for an early departure, the servicemen kept visiting with goodies. They talked of battles that they'd fought at places like Iwo Jima and Okinawa but those who'd been at Guadalcanal agreed that that had been the worst by far. They told of terrible losses at sea and how they'd fought hand to hand against the Japs for days to gain just a few feet of territory. How thousands of their buddies had been killed or died from malaria, blackwater fever and yaws. I wondered where this canal was, I'd heard of Suez and Panama but this Guadal was a new one on me. When they'd gone, we dozed off to the sound of rain drumming on the roof of the tent and the tropical insects screeching out in the jungle.

Our plane was ready to leave just after 5a.m. We were told that we'd stop at Morotai for breakfast and refuelling. Again the mighty engines swung over laboriously, caught, backfired, then settled down to the roar we'd grown accustomed to on the previous day. The plane lumbered down the runway and was airborne.

The strip at Morotai was made from marsden matting, interlocking sheets of expanded metal that had been used during the war to build airstrips in out of the way places. We were welcomed and taken into a tent where we were served toast and coffee and huge bowls of tinned peaches and cream. After breakfast I wandered over to watch a mechanic working on a fighter plane. We got chatting and I was totally oblivious of the fact that our plane was fuelled and everyone else had reboarded when the mechanic said, 'Aren't you off that Dak that's warming up its engines?'

They'd already pulled up the steps and shut the door. I ran across to the plane as one of the ground crew banged on the door. The co-pilot opened it and I scrambled up the steps before they were properly in place, jamming his fingers in the process. I don't recall what he said. Again the door was closed and latched and we headed for Darwin.

At Darwin we were again met by the Red Cross, fed generously and sent off to tent billets. We were on Australian soil at last! Once again we had a constant stream of servicemen pressing delicacies onto us. By then I'd eaten all I could possibly eat but I enjoyed the PK gum.

We left Darwin early and touched down at Cloncurry for a refuel and another hearty breakfast. As the plane climbed out of Cloncurry the temperature started to rise, and with it, the air became turbulent.

154

The plane bucked, kicked and shuddered. We encountered air pockets that caused us to drop several hundred feet and threw us about the cabin. We were all violently airsick, but the further aft we went the worse was the bucking and pitching so the sicker we became. Hoping to fly the plane above the turbulence the pilots took us up to 10 000 feet but said we couldn't go higher without oxygen. We were sure we were going to die anyway, so why not die of asphyxiation, but our reasoning was lost on those experienced fliers. The crew let us all take turns in the cockpit where the turbulence was not so noticeable and the distraction of helping fly the plane eased the nausea. From the cockpit you could look down at the apparently endless tracts of red sandy desert below us and see the glow and smoke from enormous bushfires. I'd heard about bushfires but it surprised me that Australia seemed to be all sandy desert. From what my mother told me about her girlhood in western Victoria I'd expected it to be soft rolling fields with rabbits for me to play with.

After a few hours they brought the bad news that we had to descend to 5 000 feet as we were nearing Sydney. Again the violent turbulence, again the unsteady trip to the rear of the plane and horrible retching. Billowing up from the west we could see a giant thunderstorm with jagged bolts of lightning leaping between towering clouds. The pilot said we'd have to race it to Sydney as we hadn't enough fuel to divert and the plane may not survive a run-in with a storm like that one. It was all a bit hair-raising but the plane's wheels touched the ground just as the storm's full fury hit. The lightning flashed and the thunder crashed as we ran for the terminal building.

Once again the Red Cross came to our aid. The nurses seemed shocked by our condition. A couple of them took me in their arms and I was surprised to see tears running down their cheeks as they plied us with biscuits and sweets and chocolates. They helped us with all the formalities that we were required to go through, then put us in a taxi and sent us off to the People's Palace for the night.

'Aryaztoiun'thnoit?'
'I beg your pardon.' I asked,
'Oi sed izyuz stoin th noit.'
I was nonplussed. It was morning and there was a lady at the door of the room who had a message of some sort that she wished to

convey, but I had absolutely no idea what she was trying to ask me. I sought my brother's assistance and together we ascertained that she was inquiring if it was our intention to remain another night in our room. This was my introduction to the Australian language.

After breakfast we all went across to Anthony Hordens where, courtesy of the Red Cross once again, we were outfitted with a suit of clothes each and some underwear. I got a smart grey suit with short pants and it prickled. In the afternoon, armed with the first pocket money I'd had for years, I went shopping to buy my mother a present. I walked into Woolworths and after admiring all the marvellous goods set out on the counter tops, I selected a glass bowl which was in a fixture in front of a price tag which had 2/6 written on it in red.

Now in China you *never* paid the asking price for anything. First of all it was extremely bad business as you could bargain anything down to at least half its asking price, and secondly bargaining was an accepted part of all trading. Both sides pitted their wits against each other. You'd beat the shopkeeper down to the last cent, then hand over more than the agreed price and say 'Keep the change.' It was part of the game and enjoyed by all. So I decided that I'd offer a shilling, the lady in the shop would most likely come back with a counter offer of two shillings and we'd probably settle somewhere around one and six. So, in my very best Cambridge accent, I asked the lady behind the counter what was the price of the coveted glass bowl.

'Carn yuz see its two an' six,' came the brusque reply.

'Oh that's far too much,' I replied. 'I certainly wouldn't pay any more than a shilling.'

'Yuz duzzn' hafta boi it if yuz duzzn' wannit so yuz can geddoudahere. Garn geddoud,' she snapped and walked off.

I was flabbergasted. I'd been very polite, I'd asked a price and made what was not an unreasonable offer, and I'd been ordered out of the store. Perplexed, I went back to recount this curious state of affairs to Mum who said, 'Oh Dear, you don't bargain for things in Australia.'

That was a piece of intelligence that would have been of use *before* I went shopping!

We spent several days in Sydney waiting for a place on the train to Melbourne. Folk we'd befriended showed us around the great city. One day my brother and I were taken to the Harbour Bridge by a chap who was probably in his late teens. As we were walking across the giant coat-hanger the young fellow picked me up and jokingly held me over the rail. I can still feel the terror of that moment when all there was between me and a 300-foot drop to the water was this chap's arms.

Eventually we got onto the train south which was crowded with servicemen, many of whom were on their way back to Melbourne to be discharged. We sat in the corridors with what little luggage we had and joined in the stories and the singsongs of the troops heading back to their homes. At Albury in the early hours of the morning, we changed trains onto the famous Spirit of Progress which took us on the last leg of our homeward journey.

Relations met us in Melbourne. Some I knew by name but most I didn't as I'd not seen them since I was three. A few days later we underwent thorough medical and dental examinations, our relations telling us later with much glee that they had been warned that we'd never be normal again after all we'd been through.

We went back to Colac, Mum's home town, and there recovered the condition we'd lost during the war years. When the Christmas holidays were over I was sent off to the Colac High School where my toffy accent did nothing to help me settle in. The teachers couldn't accept that a school education in China could be up to the Australian standards so I was put in with children two years younger than I, and set schoolwork that I'd done four years before. Eventually that was sorted out and I was moved up with kids of my own age. The malaria still hung around and attacked periodically for the next ten years or so.

After several months Dad came out from Hong Kong and was granted six months leave to recuperate before resuming duties in Melbourne. My brother got a job as a motor mechanic and my sister worked in the office of the Colac Dairying Company.

More than forty years later I was living in Honiara, selling and installing computers. Honiara is on Guadalcanal and no, it's not a canal it's an island, part of the Solomon Islands group off the north-eastern coast of Australia.

All around were reminders of the war. Rusted out hulks of landing barges lined the beaches and wrecks of crashed aircraft could be found in the jungle. Along the main street were painted notice boards that detailed the progress of the land battle for Guadalcanal. They recorded the tens of thousands of casualties incurred by both sides as days of hand to hand fighting yielded only a few yards of progress. On a hill overlooking the township there was a large memorial that had been erected by the Japanese Government and was often visited by Japanese who came to commemorate their dead. From time to time, aging ex US marines would fly in from the United States on pilgrimages of remembrance.

I lived on Tavio Ridge the scene of some of the most determined resistance by the Japanese troops. Shells, bullets and old helmets were often dug up in my garden and unexploded bombs were frequently found on construction sites. A friend once unearthed the remains of a Japanese soldier. My view out to sea was of Iron Bottom Sound, so named for the large number of ships that had been sunk in the campaign for the island.

One afternoon an Australian accountant, who'd been doing a consultancy job for the Solomon Islands Electricity Authority, called in to my office. We'd been talking about various matters when he asked if I'd ever lived in Hong Kong. When I replied that I had he went on to ask if I'd been a prisoner of the Japanese during World War II. Again I replied in the affirmative.

'I'm the RAAF officer' he said 'who was given the job of arranging your repatriation to Australia'.

INDEX

✳